MOUNT MARY COLLEGE LIBRARY
Milwaukee, Wisco

WITHDRAWN

W9-ASG-781

Cities of the World:

ISTANBUL

MOUNT MARY COLLEGE LIBRARY
Milwaukee, Wisconsin 53222

Cities of the World:

ISTANBUL

PETER MAYNE

with 26 photographs and 2 maps

68- 569

A. S. BARNES AND COMPANY

South Brunswick and New York

© Text, Peter Mayne, 1967

All rights reserved
Made in Great Britain
at the
Aldine Press · Letchworth · Herts
for
A. S. BARNES AND CO. INC.
Cranbury, N. J. 08512
by arrangement with
J. M. DENT & SONS LTD
Aldine House · Bedford Street · London
First published 1967

Library of Congress Catalog Card No. 67–21490

By the same author:

THE ALLEYS OF MARRAKESH
THE NARROW SMILE
THE SAINTS OF SIND
THE PRIVATE SEA

914.961
M45

Contents

List of Illustrations

(Except where otherwise stated, the photographs were taken by the author)

MAPS

Author's Note

THIS is the place the Byzantines meant when they said they lived 'in the City' or were going to it; and this is also where the Ottomans meant long before they took it, when they copied the sound of the Greek words they heard so often—εἰς τήν πόλιν ('*ees teen polin*'—'to the City')—and made it Istanbul, with Stamboul as variant. We may reasonably call it the City too. It is more than a city, more even than a capital city, though no longer a capital. Nothing that is said about it should be taken as true of Turkey as a whole. It is like a separate part of the world.

Once you leave the main lines of communication here, it is an extremely difficult place to find your way about in, let alone understand. A guide-book is absolutely essential, and this book is in no sense intended to take the place of one. It is a personal view of the City today against the visible background of its past. Anyone coming armed with prejudices different from my own will probably see it all quite differently. People looking for descriptions of the monuments should go to the specialist experts.

For those lucky enough to get hold of a copy, the best and fullest guide to the City's monuments to date, though somewhat out of date in other respects, is Ernest Mamboury's *Istanbul Touristique*, published in Istanbul. Alas, all editions, in all languages, before or post-war, are out of print. A good and readily available alternative is the 'Istanbul and Environs' section of the Hachette *Turkey*, in their World Guide series, English edition of 1960, which is based very largely on Mamboury's notes for Hachette—though he did not live to complete them. The 'Istanbul and Environs' section is also published as a separate booklet, paper covered, very handy for the pocket. Robert Liddell's altogether admirable *Byzantium and Istanbul* (London, 1956) is not a guide at all, of course, but it is excellent and very detailed on the monuments, as on all aspects of the City's past.

People seldom allow themselves enough time here. Some guide-books recognize the fact and are at pains to give a short list of the monuments that even the most hurried visitor should try to see. Hachette's *Turkey* gives such a list (page 52 of the guide, 'Visiting the Town'). If I were making my own short list, I should include several monuments Hachette's short list leaves out. My additions would be:

> The sixth-century Byzantine church of Saints Serge and Bacchus, converted into a mosque at the end of the fifteenth century as Küçük Aya Sofya Camii (Mosque of Little St Sophia).
> The sixteenth-century Ottoman mosque of Sokollu Mehmet Pasha.
> Yerebatan Saray—Constantine the Great's underground 'basilica' cistern, a splendid example of Byzantine domestic architecture, a rare commodity in the City of today.

These three monuments can easily be included in the same itinerary as St Sophia for those obliged to hurry. My fourth addition, however, is distant, difficult to get at and demands a trip to itself. It is:

> The sixteenth-century mosque of Piyalepasha—a reversion to the early Ottoman 'Bursa'-style mosque. I think it more than worth the time and trouble.

I have followed an arbitrary system of transliteration. Where a Turkish word is well known to the West I mostly use the form already familiar to us. For example, pasha, not Turkish *paşa*; kiosk, not *köşh*; odalisk, not *odalık* with its undotted 'i', a letter in Atatürk's romanized script as hopelessly confusing to the English-speaker's eye (not to mention the English type-setter's) as the sound of it is to his ear. 'The high, unrounded, inter-mediate vowel [ı] . . . does not occur in English.' [1] So I choose to ignore its separate existence, in the text as in the town plan—except where I have resolutely made it 'u' (example: 'arkaluk' on page 13 as being less ridiculously distant in sound than 'i').

---

[1] *Turkish*—in the Teach Yourself series. G. L. Lewis.

Chapter 1

A View from the Bridge

ON THE downstream side of Galata Bridge and below it there is a promenade, a sort of quay, built out well beyond the width of the upper bridge with its traffic hurtling back and forth between Stamboul the old city and Beyoğlu the new. It is at this lower level that the bath-toy steamers tie up, waiting with their white and yellow banded smoke-stacks, busy puffing out columns of cotton-wool smoke coloured anything from white to soot through sulphur. Water-buses. People crowd aboard, but in an orderly manner, the Turks being an orderly people. Though hurry seems vulgar here in the City, late-comers have to hurry for this moment in time, because the water-buses (and the trains) start on time and are apt to finish on time too. The rate of the City's pulse is seen to be deliberately slow. This is observable in the way a man leans across the parapet, or in gestures almost indolently sketched in. Gestures like action-painting on an enormous canvas might be a Turk's, perhaps an angry Turk's, but are far more likely to be a Greek's, in response to the quicker tempo of the Greek blood. The man of Greek blood and Turkish nationality the Turks still call *Rumeli*—Roman, like the citizen of Constantine the Great's New Rome. But the man in question is a Turk, talking Turkish quietly yet with a certain insistence to another, a peasant from his clothes, whose head is nod-nodding with a curious and characteristic movement like the sticking out of the neck, agreeing with whatever is being said. It is only when this second man, the peasant, raises a hand and turns to speak, slowly interrupting his friend, that his eyes suddenly let the light through from inside. He has become real, no longer an automatic man reacting to stimuli. He says—at least I think he says: 'Esquimeau-to-London-cinder. Breakneck-tent-peg bash-your-hat-in.' To which the first man replies quite calmly: 'Shindy? Bullock-larder-lair, a sorry-messiness.' The accent is strange and the cadences too lilting for English, but even so it ought all to be quite intelligible. It is nothing of the kind of course. And by now the two faces are so close that each must choose which of the two opposing eyes to focus on, as close as in rush-hour metros—not because there is no room to be otherwise, but rather as if there were a comfort, a safety, in physical nearness. Even with the people standing on your other side, along this parapet that overlooks the Golden Horn, you can sense this. Someone's anonymous elbow is against your own anonymous ribs, quite unconsciously and without pressure or movement. You move your ribs away a few inches with a vague sense of losing contact with the scene. People are standing about, not necessarily talking to each other. There is no need of talk—and anyway you can't. I cannot either, though I wish I could. Foreigners long resident in the country sometimes learn the language, though I have met many who do not seem to get much beyond kitchen talk. There was a time when even the City's non-Muslim minorities, the Greek and the Armenian and so on, did not bother to learn Turkish properly. French was then the chic language, but with independence in the air an angry campaign was launched: 'Citizen! Speak Turkish!' The minorities all speak it now, Turkish language being naturally part of the compulsory curriculum. Yet it is as axiomatic to say that foreign visitors do not speak Turkish as it is within a very few per cent of accuracy to say that Turks do not speak a second language—unless they are, for example, Turks of Kurdish blood whose second language would be Turkish, and what succour is there in this for us if we need succour? A Greek or an Armenian Turk would almost certainly speak three languages—even four, five. So looking at the crowds around you you can tell yourself for what good it will do you that say three Muslim-Turks in every hundred within sight, and perhaps three out of every four non-Muslim Turks, could understand you if you were in need of help. Which are they? We cannot even distinguish Greek from Turk in the City in the ordinary way.

But there is no crisis demanding help from others. We do not need more here than our eyes can tell us, and they light upon a small fishing boat squeezed in down below. It is fitted out with a

brazier and a great fry-pan in which something already sizzles in
the oil. The boatmen have been busy slitting and gutting fish
after fish—*palamut*, barrel-shaped, fat, iridescent, point-nosed,
shark-tailed super-mackerel cut into steaks and thrown to sizzle
in the pan along with their brothers and sisters. Then the golden
fried offerings are snapped between advertising artwork rolls for
people to breakfast off at 70 *kruş* ('kroosh') a time, not even seven-
pence. One hundred *kruş* to the Turkish *lira*, and the *lira* at present
worth ninepence in English money, about 10 cents U.S. It is not
so much that the Istanbulis like their fish fresh as that they are so
spoilt by the prodigality of their three seas—Bosphorus, Marmara
and the Golden Horn—that they will refuse it if the fish is seen
to be above a few hours out of the water, and there is not a
citizen who cannot see this for himself a mile off, the bright bold
eye, the gills flipped inside out and transformed into frilly button-
hole carnations, crimson lake. *Canli Balik*—'the living fish'—is
a popular restaurant name; and there is a popular joke restaurant
called 'The Dead Fish'. But the *rigor mortis* of the great Deep
Freeze that fascinates the West fascinates no one here where fish
is concerned. 'The Propontis has ever been renowned for an
inexhaustible store of the most exquisite fish that are taken in
their stated seasons without skill and almost without labour. . . .'
The round eighteenth-century prose style is naturally Gibbon's. [1]
'Amongst a variety of different species, the *Pelamides*, a sort of
Thunnies, were the most celebrated. . . .' He is talking of fourth-
century Byzantium, and I do not know what he means by 'most
celebrated'. Perhaps simply 'the best known'. It is an excellent
fish; and if it were less abundant it might be considered a delicacy
even here, just as the North Sea herring most certainly would be
amongst Londoners if it did not make itself so cheap.

Even so, cheap and nutritious and delicious as the *palamut*
sandwich may be, not everybody on this bridge can afford to buy
himself a breakfast at all. Make your way to the other side of the
bridge and you will see. An arched passage-way under the traffic,
past kiosks for cigarettes or fresh fruit juices or a thinned yoghourt drink called *ayran* much sought after in summer, iced and
salted. If it is a cold day you can have *boza* instead, or a wonderful

[1] *Decline and Fall of the Roman Empire*: available in the Everyman Edition.

hot *salep*. Go on past the tea-shops and steamer-ticket booths and a useful board of steamer times and destinations. You will find, at balmy seasons of the year, whole groups of men with fishing-lines dropped between adjacent skiffs or else from the decks of the smaller Golden Horn water-buses resting quietly between one zigzag trip upstream and the next. It does not take long to learn that, since there is no hurry, by far the most agreeable means of getting about and seeing the City's broad view and the most beautiful waterway in the world, the Bosphorus, is by water-bus. It is as if the City loved her seas as they love her, and was at pains always to look her best for them.

The fishers are intent, and possessed of patience, though they do not have to use much of it. Small fish called *istravit*, or with luck *uskumru* (a member of the mackerel family much smaller and finer than the *palamut*) are obligingly ready to get themselves hooked in return for a shred of shrimp, even of mussel. At the cost of an hour not otherwise committed anyway, a man with hooks and a line and as many shrimp shreds as he counts mouths at home to feed, can feed them all a modest breakfast—but he would need a very long line for *uskumru*, because this fish feeds deep. The Golden Horn is very deep just here, and this is doubt-less why they floated Galata Bridge (and Atatürk Bridge upstream of it, for that matter) on huge iron pontoons. Both bridges open briefly during the black hours before dawn to let shipping through a swinging centre-section. Civil commotion also causes them to open like a sort of fire-break, isolating the two parts of the City.

Time is not money here: it is infinitely more precious. Spare time. 'Let the cares of tomorrow be forgotten,' the Turks say. There are plenty of men who live somehow without working much. In fact there is a category of 'worker' the Turkish statis-ticians have specially invented in their breakdown of figures for the population in employment or looking for it: 'Those not having broken with their normal occupations.' I take this to mean those who are enjoying time off from work in a random sort of way, depending upon the weather and their mood; as here perhaps—the weather perfect, the mood tranquil.

Here on the bridge it is an almost exclusively male society tranquilly enjoying the perfect weather, and many are just watching the labours of those who fish. Quite a lot of the men with lines are clearly rich enough to buy a dozen breakfasts (the necktie, the solid shoes, the solid suit) and choosy enough not to choose *uskumru* at this season—which I shall make autumn, because I hold autumn to be the loveliest time of all in the City. However, autumn is too early for *uskumru* to be at its best. 'Never eat *uskumru* except when the snows are falling.' I quote a Turkish lady connoisseur I was to meet later. She has also announced: 'Never eat red mullet in London.' When taxed about this she explains that Londoners may eat it there if they cannot taste for themselves that it is uneatable from northern waters. She has never been to New York and so cannot make any firm pronouncement about American red mullet ('have they even got it?') though she would confidently expect it to be uneatable.

But whether you eat your catch or throw it back into the depths of the Golden Horn, or reserve it for such as you may meet of the City's immense cat population, whom it is everybody's duty to love and feed, or whether you just watch others at it, there is a sense of slow pure joy on these floating slap-water quays. The Istanbulis love this bridge. How did Louis MacNeice miss it all? Was it his preoccupation with history?

> . . . Too much history
> Tilting, canting, crawling, rotting away. . . .[1]

When poets are dispassionate, however, there is no poetry. But no one, not being a poet, has ever been dispassionate about this city either, loving it or hating it recklessly. Perhaps he too went whizzing across the bridge with the commuter ants at breakfast time and back again at dusk so that all he saw was

> . . . too many dark cloth caps
> On the conveyor-belt that twice a day
> Spans the Golden Horn . . .
> . . . while the sky . . .
> . . . sags like a tent . . .

[1] From a poem, 'Constant', from *Collected Poems*, by Louis MacNeice, by permission of Faber & Faber Ltd and Oxford University Press, New York; copyright © The Estate of Louis MacNeice, 1966.

So he probably never knew, as the Turks have always known and those with a mind to can learn for themselves, that there is a word for this sort of pleasure, the sort that is quiet but keen, bringing extravagant rewards at the cost of almost no effort—and what could be more elegant than that? The word is *keyif*. Rich and poor fishers and standers-by, they are all at present in an euphoric state of *keyif*. No government inquiry is needed here into the problems of leisure. Leisure does not create problems in this city, it solves them. A newcomer might well try freeing his mind of any outside rubbish that may be cluttering it and do as the citizens do, one of the many things to be done in a crowd, with or without companions. Go to the bridge and fish a bit; or if too indolent to fish, then watch a bit; and then perhaps wander across a blank like a bomb site to a small fish market under its corrugated roofing near by that I have read of as 'sordid', though for me it is a magnet. It is filled with fish as brilliant as the flowers in their stated seasons, all displayed on deep red and green painted platters. There is *kalkan* ('the shield'—turbot to us); *dil* ('the tongue'—sole to us); *levrek* (sea bass); there is *kiliç* ('the sword', for sword-fish) and many, many others, some with wings like spiky cat-sized butterflies, and king of them all for many, a fish uniquely Bosphorus, the bluish *lüfer*, for which no one else has a name except the ichthyologists (temnodon). Shellfish squirm (shrimps) and wriggle (giant prawns) and snap their fan-tails as if to shoot backwards through the air as once, poor things, they torpedoed backwards through the water (lobsters big and small, and I do not mean *langoustes*, though they are here too). Some of the shrimps, the best and the most expensive, are so small that one wonders who will have the patience to shell them, and whether grilled on a hot-plate they might not comfortably go down whole. They do. Let the newcomer look and envy. All this he can do as a first lesson in *keyif* on his first morning in the City, before the monuments are open.

Veils of mist lie softly on the waters still, a sort of yashmak of autumnal opalescence that still conceals the face of the old city on the farther side. The mists will be rising by nine or half past, a lifting of the veils. On the high points of a modest undulating ridge a great march of imperial monuments takes shape

triumphantly, a procession that recedes and comes forward, dips
to the water's edge and soars again, in absolute dominion over the
roofs that eddy like a waterfall about the great ones' feet. The eye
follows, led by this ritual progress from one giant stepping-stone
to the next across the roof tops. A palace on the point, and no one
needs to be told that it is the Grand Seraglio, Topkapi Saray,
its tower like an Anglican church steeple showing above heavy
trees. Then the sixth-century Byzantine church of St Irene; and
then the dome and minarets of St Sophia, recognized from a
thousand picture postcards; and beyond that the points of the
Blue Mosque's six thin minarets—the eye could miss this if not
on the look-out for it. Next an intruder (how did it elbow its way
up here?), institutionally red, grey, horizontal, topped by shallow
towers—a boys' *lycée*, and we can skip it quickly, hurrying on to
the eighteenth-century Nuruosmaniye Mosque beyond, nor
stopping there long either before coming down to another
mosque infinitely superior, and more clearly seen down by the
water at the far end of the bridge—the Yeni Validé (the New
Queen Mother's Mosque. Completed 1663). Pigeons fly up outside
this mosque in a vast wheeling concourse, just as pigeons fly up
in the Piazza San Marco in Venice and for the same good reason,
scared from their grain by something. There is merit in offering
them grain here (and none in eating them, nor much pleasure
either). The eye soars with them, and beyond—to the University
'fire-watching' tower on the skyline, missing on the way, almost
certainly, one of the City's finest mosques, Rüstem Pasha's
(*c.* 1560), too small and dark in its shadows to compete with the
immense imperial splendours of the grandest of them all that
rises up against the sky, the Suleimaniye Mosque (1557). So
compelling is the Suleimaniye that another huge mosque, half
seen to the left of the tower, will probably not be noticed at all,
though it is the Mosque of Beyazit (completed 1505) and much
worth going to. It is the earliest mosque to be built in what was
to develop into the sixteenth-century Imperial Ottoman style.
  In this panorama it is the lovely Aqueduct of Valens that ought
by rights to make the horizontal counterbalance to the curve of
domes, the recurrent vertical of minarets, but alas it is not visible
from here, being hidden in the fold of land between the Third

B

and Fourth of Constantine's Seven Hills of New Rome that it
was designed to bridge; but to the right of where it is concealing
itself is the great Fatih ('Conqueror's') Mosque (rebuilt 1771),
dwarfing the domes of the Mollazeyrek Mosque (once the Byzantine church of the Saviour Pantocrator) below it. And at this
point a warehouse juts out from the near-side shores, stopping
the eye with concrete and dusty window-panes.

It is probably time in any case to get on with the day. There
will be no stopping a bus, or a taxi, or a taxi-*dolmuş* (a 'stuffed'
taxi; stuffed, that is, with passengers each paying his fixed share).
A fat fine awaits anyone who tries to pick up a fare on the bottle-
neck of a bridge. So cross on foot. In crossing, moreover, you
will get the better of the warehouse that cut the panorama short.
Another great mosque comes into view on the right; more simple,
even austere; it is Sultan Selim I's (1522), and it rates very high
with the experts. To its right again a minor horror, the great
grey pepper-pot of a Greek college, ugly nineteenth-century
institutional again, but never mind; it can be put to use as a
pointer. Almost immediately below it is a ninth-century Byzantine church otherwise easily missed, quite near the water. This
was once the Church of St Theodosia, now the Gül Camii, or
'Rose Mosque'. And working from the pepper-pot again, to the
right, a skeleton on the distant skyline in which sharp eyes will
pick out empty eye-sockets. Something abandoned? A factory?
And beside it, what? Something high and formless. The Palace
of Constantine Porphyrogenitus—Tekfursaray: and beside that
two crumbling towers of the Theodosian land walls.

The Golden Horn now curves out of sight, making for the
Sweet Waters of Europe that earlier generations loved so. The
sultans had a favourite pavilion there; their subjects would come
picnicking, the two segregated sexes making eyes at each other
at a distance. The ladies also made eyes at their boatmen (then
mostly Greeks) and the boatmen made them back discreetly, and
no doubt there was a lot of sighing and minute immodest ges-
turing. Today the same two sexes would find the waters less
sweet than they remembered them, not to say stagnant, and all
built around.

The mosque and tomb of Eyüp, the Prophet's Standard-Bearer,

are crouched in the distance, and beyond them the little café on a hill where Pierre Loti used to sit as the sun was setting—but the newcomer would have to take all this on trust or, better still, go there in the evening. For the moment there is the business of a taxi; but he will have discovered meanwhile that from this bridge down in the true guts of the waterfront all these are not just monuments suspended in a vacuum, they are integral parts of life here, that life is a warm reality, the euphoria of *keyif* is not a waste of time where time is not money nor money the yardstick, and that anyone who cares to share it will be a first step towards understanding this strange and magnificent city.

Chapter 2

Cosmopolis

'ISTANBUL is a cosmopolitan city. . . .'

It always has been, both under the Byzantine and the Ottoman empires, and perhaps this is the moment to remind ourselves that there never was a Turkish empire. Under the sultans the 'best people' were Osmanlis, members of the House of Osman— Ottoman, as we are accustomed to say. But in fact during the Ottoman golden period only one of the best people counted at all, the Best Person himself, the sultan—and there was no question of his being the Grand Turk the West thought him. *Türk*, to Ottoman ears, was a term of disparagement. Anatolian peasants were Turks. Loutish. Clods. No. The Ottoman Sultan was 'by the grace of God King of Kings, Lord of Lords, Greatest Emperor of Constantinople and Trapizond, most mighty King of Persia, Arabia, Syria, Egypt, Lord of Asia and Europe, Prince of Mecha and Aleppo, Ruler of Jerusalem and Master of the Universall Sea' —which is how Sultan Suleiman the Magnificent was styled in English translation, with no sense of its being offensive to call Istanbul 'Constantinople' as there is among Turks today, just as in Greece it is equally offensive to call it 'Istanbul'.

By the mid sixteenth century the sultan's City numbered half a million souls (of which, incidentally, Gibbon claims that the 'Moslems were less numerous . . . than Christians or even Jews'), and this at a time when Queen Elizabeth I of England was throwing up her hands in horror at being told that the City of London's population had rocketed to 98,000. To Suleiman London must have sounded a modest little township; certainly Queen Elizabeth was for him, decently, yes, but very modestly 'Most Honourable Matrone of the Christian Religion, Mirror of Chastity'.

The census for 1965 gives the City a total of 2,302,438 souls, and it is the Turkish State Planning organization who must now

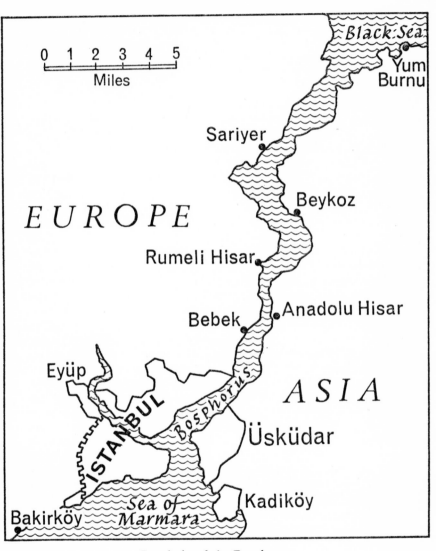

Istanbul and the Bosphorus

throw up their hands in horror at their own estimates of four millions by 1980.

Istanbul is a cosmopolitan city . . . A quarter of the population is non-Turkish and non-Muslim. These elements either enjoyed the protection of the Capitulations or have breathed the atmosphere of those that did so and have assumed their mentality. In spite of the twenty-five-odd years that have passed since the abolition of the Capitulations, they have never been erased from the minds of this class.

I quote from Geoffrey Lewis's *Turkey* in the Nations of the World series.[1] He is citing, in translation, an extract from the *Idare Dergisi* (official journal of Administration of the Ministry of the Interior). With independence *kosmopolit*, not *Türk*, was to become the rude word. 'Turk-disparagement' had become an offence in law. Minorities were welcome as citizens but must learn to watch their p's and q's now that the protection of the great powers had been withdrawn from them along with the Capitulations.

The City could easily become one of the world's great tourist attractions; it is in fact—though it cannot be said to have equipped itself to play the role professionally as yet. Development schemes are in hand. The State's 1963–7 Five-Year Plan made provision for them. Investors in touristic fields such as new hotels or restaurants or places of entertainment are offered handsome ten-year remissions of tax. Batches of young men have been sent to Belgium to study various branches of the 'industry', in particular hotel-keeping and tourist agency work, and so on. By 1966 results were only just starting to come off the production line.

This unprofessionalism meanwhile makes things in many ways especially agreeable for those who come visiting. The City is unspoilt; touts do not lie in wait for the innocent, nobody yet realizes that we visitors could be his breakfast, lunch and dinner. But it also makes it difficult for those who look for more than a brisk organized whirl round the City in a tourist bus. The whole idea of 'tourism' in the public mind has yet to reach the point where, for example, it would be socially respectable for citizens with the requisite high standards of education (including at least

[1] London, 1955.

two European languages) to consider 'guiding' as a serious profession. There can be no double standards where guides are concerned; a guide is no good at all unless he is very good indeed.
In default of very good indeed a good guide-book is better. But
quite apart from the monuments and what they stand for, there
are also the practical problems—finding the way, finding the
place open when you get there. Opening and closing days and
times vary according to season, summer and winter, and also
according to which of the four different authorities controlling
things is concerned. Mosques will be open at prayer times, by no
means always at other times, and many visitors may feel timid
about disturbing other people at prayer, though no Muslim will
mind, provided the visitor removes his shoes and behaves as he
would in his own place of worship.

From the bridge the skyline was in complete control of the
old city; on the town plans two 'seas' and the land walls, plus
the imposition of certain key thoroughfares like sabre-cuts
across it, reinforce the impression of discipline and order. But
lower than the skyline, deeper than the sabre-cuts—inside in
fact—everything is fluid, following the dictates not of man but
of a terrain whose configuration we cannot grasp once it is all
around us, so overlaid is it with haphazard building. To reduce it
to order is impossible, and to write about it in an ordered fashion
almost as impossible. Time seems to go backwards and forwards,
coexists, space expands, contracts, the wood hides itself resolutely
behind the trees. Street corners can form the acutest of angles,
so that the houses on them stick out like the sharp end of a
slice of cake. It does not help much to conclude that this was
once the junction of two streams, dry now, and hemmed in with
little shop fronts, filled with people, merchandise, pack-animals,
men with push-carts, a street porter carrying something crated—
a grand piano? I cling to an observable fact. To carry a crated
piano I must first of all have a thing called an *arkaluk*, a fat, two-
foot, two-faced letter 'b' of stuffed leather, carpet-covered, fitted
with shoulder-harness like a rucksack. I now stand, bent almost
double, to the point where my shoulders and the bulb of the 'b'
together describe a horizontal line along which the load will
distribute itself evenly in a minute. I am loaded by friends who

grunt and heave, and since this is a biggish load a cord from the far front end of the crate is put into my hand to help with the balancing. I hang on with this hand, leaving the other swinging free to the ground in a marionettish manner. I now set off and cause havoc, but I also provoke the instant compassion of any tourist who sees me so red in the face and panting. I reject his compassion instantly and absolutely. Does the wretch not know that I am of Kurdish blood, and that my forbears were obliged to kill off the City's Armenians in 1896 precisely so that they might wrest the virtual monopoly in street porterage from them? Kurds are very proud of their weight-carrying powers, and are right to be. So was Sultan Murat IV (1623–40) proud of his; and he would show it off by picking up a couple of great hefty henchmen and larking around Topkapi Saray with them both held aloft. We even know the names of two such who were so treated—Melek Ahmet and Musa. Evliya Çelebi tells us about it in his *Narrative of Travels in Europe, Asia and Africa*.[1] Çelebi is well worth reading, and is excellently presented to the general public by A. A. Pallis in his *In the Days of the Janissaries*,[2] which edits a text that could do with editing, and amplifies it richly for us. Anyway, it was nothing for Sultan Murat to pick up his pages too, and spin them in the air in a prankish sort of way that terrified them and caused Evliya Çelebi himself (an inner-circle page at the time) to squeal out: 'For God's sake, my Emperor! I am quite giddy.' The sultan laughed, put him down and gave him forty-eight gold sequins for his pains, so it was well worth a squeal or two.

But in the public streets outsize load-carrying certainly does tend to obstruct, and cobbles on hills do not help us, though they seem to help rubber-shod ponies. Alleyway name plaques, where they exist, are not always easy to spot; not that it matters for anyone just wandering—on the contrary, anywhere in the old city is fascinating and often instructive, if there is time to wander. But is there? And we arrive at the time-factor that so bedevils visitors in a hurry here.

[1] Translated by von Hammer, a great historian of the Ottoman Empire, London, 1846–50.
[2] London, 1951.

An English friend, whose intimate knowledge of the monuments very often involves her in showing visiting friends around,
has observations to make about their reactions and the time it all
takes. Scholars are easy, she says; they know exactly what they
want to see, and even if there is no hurry are not to be enticed
away from their purpose by anything extraneous to it. With the
ordinary non-specialist newcomer it can be very different. The
more intelligent his interest, the more hopelessly can he get
bogged down in side-issues. It takes not less than a month to get
round the City properly. The average visitor, so statistics tell
us, may spend five days in Turkey as a whole—would that mean
two in the City? Certainly not more than three. To cover a
cross-section of the best in so short a time demands a carefully
planned programme and the self-discipline not to be enticed
away from it by every novelty that presents itself in a city of
experiences novel to us. I quote this same friend here on something else as well—that certain of the greatest monuments should
be seen before certain others. The most cogent example is the
Kahriye Museum (Church of St Saviour in Chora), which should
be seen before St Sophia. The point is valid. No one can fail to
find the Kahriye's mosaics and frescoes breath-taking, not to
speak of the marbles. It is enough to use the eyes. But on first
going into St Sophia, that building so infinitely more wonderful,
the same intelligently interested newcomer may be disappointed
if his knowledge, sense of history and conditioned emotional
responses do not fill in for him what his eyes are missing. Is St
Sophia perhaps too huge to be so empty? This may be the first
shock; the tragic, dead emptiness, which I realize myself in retro-
spect can trouble the mind in a way that does not at once explain
itself. But if the newcomer had already seen the Kahriye, and
taken conscious note of what meticulous restitution can do (the
City owes the Kahriye's restitution to the Byzantine Institute of
Boston, U.S., who deserve the highest praise), his imagination
could better reconstruct St Sophia with its marbles cleaned, its
dome, semi-domes, apse, galleries, narthex, exonarthex all glittering and golden, brilliant with mosaic. The great pavement,
strewn since the Fall in 1453 with carpets and prayer-rugs, was
strewn with worshippers as well till 1935, when Atatürk ordained

that St Sophia should henceforth be offered to the world as a
museum. So museum it is, full now of us with cameras, busy
snapping the unsnappable; for while our eyes have wide peri-
pheral vision and our heads turn on our necks so that we take in
the whole great edifice's extent in a single panoramic glance,
our cameras can see only what is presented to them within the
limits of perhaps a forty-five degree angle; and to use a wide-
angle lens is to cause the columned galleries to totter and threaten
to fall out sideways.

This vast pavement, now bare, was once '. . . like the sea . . .
for certain blue waves are raised up against the stone, much as
though you had cast a pebble into water and disturbed its calm'.
Michael of Thessalonika recorded this in the twelfth century.
Looking up from the pavement to the dome 180 feet above it,
even today with the golden splendour gone, who does not still
wonder how it can float so light and free? Yet there seems to be a
disarmingly simple reason why this should be as nearly as any
architect has yet contrived 'the airborne vault of the universe'.
Robert Liddell [1] cites it: it is because the dome 'rests everywhere
on sharply receding surfaces'. But if for some newcomer it is not
enough when first he is confronted by the bare undecorated bones
of St Sophia (the exposed mosaics are magnificent, of course, but
so few, in relation to the huge empty wall spaces), then he is in
good company. Neither did bare bones satisfy the Byzantines.

It may be that some sort of running order should be considered
in the seeing of Ottoman mosques as well as of Byzantine churches.
A newcomer is unlikely to have any critical standards to apply to
the hundreds of mosques to be seen on all sides. It takes a little
time to get an unaccustomed eye in. This is true not only of the
mosques. Everything here takes time. It ought all to be approached
slowly, obliquely, rather as a Turk (and perhaps an Englishman)
approaches friendship with a stranger. Some hearts are not worn
on the sleeve. So if anyone has taken the suggestion seriously
that he might linger on the bridge some early morning, then there
is something else worth doing, another deliberate slowing down
of the approach, in this case a detour on the way to St Sophia via

[1] *Byzantium & Istanbul*, London, 1956.

the Kahriye. It requires a taxi, or a car, and the route can be followed on the town plan on pages 34–5.

The detour starts out on the new Florya Sahil Yolu (Florya Sea-front Road) beyond the commotions of the railway terminus at Sirkeci, where the 'Stamboul Express' comes home to roost (though it has changed its name). It follows along outside the old sea walls of Byzantium, on land only recently reclaimed—a fine road. Topkapi Saray sprawls above on its wooded promontory. The railway keeps pace inside the walls, but life has encroached on the narrow space between the rail tracks and the walls themselves, worming its way into them, on to them, over them. Cottages, shacks, have become part of their fabric and now grow out of them, along with the creepers and flowers that residents have planted to give themselves shade and pleasure. The Turks have always loved flowers. Their ceramic tiles are covered with them—carnations, wild hyacinths, tulips and the rest. It was from sixteenth-century Turkey that tulips were first introduced to the West. Our name for them—tulip—is itself a corruption of a Turkish word we thought meant 'turban', but really meant the muslin winder round the base of some turbans (*dülbend*). Tulips gave their name to one of the City's mosques, though not, I think, one of the best: the Laleli Camii (1763). The Turks call the tulip *lale*, not 'turban'. Tulips gave their name to a reign too, that of Sultan Ahmet III (1703–30), who had a passion for them and would give tulip fêtes in the season. Tortoises with lit candles stuck on their backs would bulldoze in and out amongst the flowers to the delight of everybody. Tulip bulbs in our day are laid out for sale on street corners at planting time.

Here on the sea walls, where windows peer between the crenellations, and balconies have somehow managed to fasten themselves on outside, and potted plants abound, it is mostly plants that give a longer showing for the money than tulips. It is all very pleasant, and very much a place for people to come to of a summer evening, to one or other of the cafés, or to eat in some rough little eating-house on the sea front. The level is strictly popular just here.

Some way along the road a Byzantine palace stares down from its three remaining corbelled windows at first-floor level. The embrasures are marble still, but to left and right there is little more than crumbling masonry. This is the Palace of the Boucoleon (sometimes called the Palace of Justinian). A vast complex of palaces once covered the slopes of the First Hill of New Rome grouped alongside and below St Sophia and the Hippodrome, but except for this modest façade practically every vestige of the other palaces has disappeared—the Porphyry Palace, the Chalke, the Daphne, the Chrysotriclinion and the rest, though several fine tessellated pavements (? eleventh century) are still to be seen where once stood the Sacred Palace and now stands the little Mosaics Museum.

John Tzimisces came by boat quietly under the walls of the Palace of the Boucoleon one December night of the year 969. The Emperor Nicephoros Phocas and his Empress Theophano were in residence; she was expecting this visit, he was not. If, as some said, it was baskets that her serving maids let down (perhaps from these very windows) to pull up John Tzimisces and his murder party in, then they must have been robust maidens; but Gibbon says it was ladders and ropes and not baskets they used. It sounds on the whole more likely. Anyway the murderers were soon inside and the emperor successfully slaughtered, after some preliminary torturing. His severed head was then slung out of the window into the sea. This done, John was free to marry his mistress the widowed empress, and to occupy the cuckold's throne as well as his bed.

It must be said in the Empress Theophano's defence that the Emperor Nicephoros Phocas, who was accustomed to being greeted with a hymn of praise starting 'Behold the Morning Star approaches', was absolutely hideous. Liutprand, who had come with an embassy from Otto of Savoy only the year before the murder, describes him for us: 'A monstrosity of a man, a dwarf, fat-headed, with tiny mole's eyes, disfigured by a neck scarcely an inch long, pig-like by reason of the big close bristles on his head . . .' He was dirty and foul-smelling into the bargain. Probably the empress could bear it no longer.

The Boucoleon was a huge palace, though today it has only these few gaping windows to show for it. I suppose I have quoted Liutprand's description of the murdered emperor largely in the hope that it may serve to fill out a bit the little that our eyes can see.

On the far side of the groyne immediately beyond the Palace
of the Boucoleon a dome and a minaret are visible above the
walls. It is the Küçük Aya Sofya Camii (Mosque of little St Sophia
—once church of SS. Serge and Bacchus—sixth century). It is
extremely beautiful and should be high on anybody's priority
list. This glance in passing will establish its location for when the
time comes to visit it.

At intervals along the sea front there will have been glimpses of
important monuments, apart from Topkapi Saray—St Irene, for
example, and St Sophia with its great clumsy ochrous lateral
buttressing, a heavy silhouette, but so charged with meaning that
its external heaviness is disregarded. The ochre buttresses are
contemporaneous with the sixth-century building; the other
buttresses are later Byzantine, or Ottoman, added as often as
earthquakes or other misfortunes threatened the structure. People
are accustomed to say that the Byzantines cared little about the
external appearance of their churches, but I cannot help thinking
that if they had managed to solve the problem of giving exterior
support to an immense high dome without such cumbrousness,
they would have been quick to use the knowledge. The Ottomans
did find a solution a thousand years later, and as far as exteriors
are concerned this can be easily verified by comparing St Sophia's
with that of Sultan Ahmet's Blue Mosque (1616) near by. Surely
even a militantly loyal Christian will admit that the latter is in
elegant and composed equilibrium and that St Sophia is not,
even if he closes the eye of faith to the added buttresses? Inside,
however, as even a militant Turk will agree, the situation is
reversed. Are we to suppose, then, that the architect Mehmet
Ağa did not know how to cause his 'Blue Mosque's' dome to
float as light and free as St Sophia's, where he could surely see for
himself how it was to be done? Was it, perhaps, that he deliberately equated grandeur with a certain measured weightiness (an
Ottoman characteristic, incidentally, in practically everything
they touched)? Or is the explanation to be found in purely func-
tional considerations? As Robert Liddell and others have pointed
out, Byzantine church ritual demanded a processional approach
to the altar—to which the basilica form, with arched galleries
right and left of the aisle, is exactly suited. Islamic ritual demands

the greatest available width giving unbroken sight-lines on the *mihrab* (the praying-niche orientated on Mecca), so that the greatest number of worshippers can enjoy positions in the front rank. We may think of the Byzantines as advancing on the altar like a regiment in column of route, of the Muslims as a regiment standing, kneeling, prostrating itself in line behind the prayer leader. In any event Mehmet Ağa's dome (72 feet in diameter— St Sophia's is 101 feet) is borne up on four elephantine fluted columns (16 feet in diameter). In this way he successfully opens up the ground space laterally, but forces upon us the visual impression that his dome must be of monstrous weight to have need of such monstrous internal supporters. The 'Blue Mosque' is easy to visit along with St Sophia and is open all day, but it should not be the only Ottoman mosque a visitor gives himself time to go into. Despite the blue ceramic tiling inside, that gives the mosque the name we know it by (some of it very fine, some very far from fine), the best of the mosque is visible from outside, and it is very remarkable. Yet it already seems to presage the Ottoman decline, in which architecture was to follow the sultans themselves from their apogee down to rock bottom and the grave.

At the moment of writing the Florya Sea Road does not yet get as far as the bathing-beaches of Florya that it seemed to be promising us; until quite recently it did not even reach the land walls and the old fortress of Yedikule ('Seven Towers'). It petered out suddenly. It was a project of President Menderes's that died with his own downfall and death and has only lately been resuscitated. The road already rounds the land walls on the Marmara and by the time this is in print will have reached the promised land. But in any event we shall be turning into the City at Atatürk Boulevard and making fixedly for the first roundabout.

Hitherto we have caught distant sight of many mosques, but only one at close quarters—the Mosque of the Yeni Validé at Galata Bridge, a very fine one indeed. We are about to have ringside seats for a view of the ultimate horror mosque. It stands immediately beyond the roundabout, and was thought up in 1871 for the queen mother of the time by a fashionable Italian architect. You are invited to give it a long withering look as we round the roundabout. This is a piece of deliberate prophylaxis—

so look, and inoculate yourself against the like for ever more. It
is the Validé Mosque at Aksaray. Prim, overdressed, bourgeois;
decoration like costume jewellery thrown on in a wanton fit;
minarets too fat for the hypodermic needles they resemble, too
thin for muezzins (unless very small, thin muezzins, children
possibly). It is awful, in the absolute sense: you are not allowed to
say 'tastes differ' or that 'tastes change'. It is thoroughly bad of
its kind, and the fact of its being a place of worship must not
oblige us to shut up about it.

After the Validé at Aksaray it will be clear why the Yeni Validé
Mosque at Galata Bridge is filled with virtue and not just big;
and, later in the day, clear why the mosque of Sokollu Mehmet
Pasha, for example, is better still and not just small. Make now
for the land walls at the far end of Vatan Caddesi.

Even today the ruined walls are wonderful, still capable of
suggesting the riches they were put up to defend. They give scale
moreover. The City's old Byzantine identity becomes plainer to
anyone who has driven along in the shadow of these walls. Here
in the City there is so little visual evidence left of all that public
splendour so long ago. What is there now to prove that nowhere
in the contemporary world for a period of seven hundred years
at least were such riches to be seen in the streets; such sculpture,
palaces, luxury shops, promenades, such a hippodrome, such
elaboration of costume and jewellery? And what of the air they
breathed?

At Edirne Gate leave the land walls and turn back into the City.
Do not let a big mosque to the right distract you; the destination
for the moment is the Kahriye Museum, to the left, inside the
walls, quite close by. In what was once the Church of St Saviour
in Chora, in its mosaics and frescoes, its marbles, the air of Byzantium is palpable, all-pervading. When their world had already
split in two, and the heavens seemed to be falling about their
ears, the Byzantines still had the faith and the strength and the
passion to be capable of this astonishing fourteenth-century
renaissance in the realm of religious art. Here it seems easier for
the ordinary twentieth-century mortal to understand the ordinary
Byzantine citizen's everyday concern with theological dogma.

Within a year of the foundation of the City the First Oecumenical Council, of Niceae (A.D. 325), had settled for him the torturing problem of the true nature of Christ. No one any longer had need to fret himself with such questions as: 'Since He is the Son of God, then is He not younger than God. . . ? [Arius] did not deny the Godhead of Christ, but he did make Him inferior to the Father —of *like* substance, not of the *same* substance, which was the view held by Athanasius, and stamped as orthodox by the Council of Niceae.' [1] But with that controversy settled, there were plenty of others to exercise the citizen's mind, e.g. the Iconoclasts versus the Iconodules. By his decree banning the worship of images the Emperor Leo III struck his blow for the Iconoclasts, though this is not to be seen as a purely theological problem. The Iconoclast emperors were intent upon curtailing the power of the Church; it was the Church that owned the sacred icons and the sacred icons that brought the citizens in to worship.

And it was the Iconodules who won the day. The citizens had daily need of their churches and their icons, and it is in the frescoes and mosaics of the Kahriye that we can see not only what holy persons looked like to the Byzantines but also how they saw one another. Theodore Metochite, the benefactor of this church, kneels before Christ Enthroned in one of the mosaics, for instance.

The impact of this place is powerful in the extreme and of a profound but melancholy beauty. Perhaps this comment would be true of the City as a whole.

St Saviour in Chora is sixth-century, much restored in the twelfth and thirteenth, and it was not turned into a mosque for some fifty years after the Fall—by Sultan Beyazit II's Grand Vizier Atikali Pasha, at the end of the fifteenth century. This Grand Vizier was a eunuch. He was not a vandal, however; he did not think it necessary to destroy the mosaics simply because of their Christian content, he merely had them put out of sight behind plaster. St Sophia was allowed to display its mosaics till the eighteenth century. Perhaps the Kahriye seemed so relatively small

---

[1] *Alexandria. A History and a Guide*. E. M. Forster. Available as an Anchor Original.

1. The old city, Stamboul, from the Sea of Marmara, showing the six minarets of Sultan Ahmet's 'Blue' Mosque, and to the right of it, St Sophia. Seraglio Point, far right.

2. Under Galata Bridge. Golden Horn water-buses and the quiet pleasures of the waterfront.

Total relaxation in the sun (*page 111*).

]4. An open-air fish market, the
ıleimaniye Mosque in background.
ťosque of Rüstem Pasha partly
ŝible on right.

]5. Three of the city's cat population
ɔnfidently awaiting fish scraps.

. Fish for breakfast (*page 4*).▷

7. An accouchement in the Harem.
'Oh, let it be a male child!'

8. Interior of a Harem. The architect Melling's
proposed design for his patron, *Hadijé Sultane*,
sister of Sultan Selim III. It was never built, but
nevertheless shows better than anything else
available how an imperial princess of the early
nineteenth century may have seen herself and her
entourage. Note a eunuch in centre foreground.

9. Peasants turned citizens, in front of the Yeni Validé Mosque.

10, 11. To feed the pigeons with grain is meritorious . . . to scare them off is less so. ▷

12. The seesaw is its own reward. ▷

13. The sultan goes forth on a ceremonial occasion (*page 53*).

14. Life-size nineteenth-century mannequins of Janissaries in the Askeri Museum. Here shown: a Çorbaci, or 'soup-man', on the left; a Sakabaşi, or 'chief water-carrier', on the right (*page 72*).

that its mosaics would be too present, too close, for the faithful to pray in peace, watched over by Our Lord and His disapproving saints.

The return to the centre of the old city will be down Fevzi Pasha Caddesi, a road that will change its name several times before we get there. There is quite a lot to notice in passing, on the way. The biggish mosque just inside the Edirne Gate will be an excellent corrective after the Validé. It is the Mihrimah (*c.* 1558), and by a master, Sinan, though it cannot be rated among his finest work. It is shaped like a huge lantern, a fact I find less interesting than that Mihrimah was Sultan Suleiman the Magnificent's daughter by Roxelana, and had been married off to one Rüstem Pasha. In natural consequence Rüstem became Grand Vizier as soon as the post was made vacant by the assassination of the previous incumbent—one Ibrahim. This was plain sewing for Roxelana. The sultan was as putty in her hands and readily agreed, despite his long and intimate association with Ibrahim, who as a slave boy had been the companion of his youth, both in and out of bed, so many were to whisper at the time. But Busbecq, who came as ambassador to Istanbul from the Holy Roman Empire during Suleiman's reign (1520–66), and was to publish his *Travels into Turkey*, etc.,[1] thought differently. He made it his business to inquire into all manner of things at court, and wrote of the sultan: 'In his younger days he was not given to wines, nor to masculine venery, which the Turks much delight in.' In any event Ibrahim was out, and Rüstem was in. We have already had a sight of the mosque the same Sinan was to build for Rüstem (*c.* 1560). It is small and beautiful and contains some of the best ceramic tiling in the City.

Sinan the Architect is to sixteenth-century Istanbul what Sir Christopher Wren was to seventeenth-century London, and we have now noted three of his mosques: the Suleimaniye, Rüstem Pasha, Mihrimah. On the way to St Sophia we shall see a fourth, the Şehzadé. Already the Sinan sign manual will be getting familiar. The Şehzadé stands on the left of the road a little beyond the Byzantine Aqueduct of Valens (so thoroughly restored by the

---

[1] London, 1744, in translation from the Latin.

ubiquitous Sinan that it is thought of as an Ottoman monument).
The Şehzadé Mosque was built at Suleiman's command in
memory of a beloved son, 'Prince Mehmet, who died at a very
young age'—so a municipal tourist hand-out informs us. But
here again, Busbecq (and others) would beg to differ, or in any
case give the comment a certain twist. For Suleiman seems to
have built the mosque in remorseful recognition of his guilt in
the assassination of his first-born, Mustafa (not Mehmet?), by a
former harem favourite called Bosfor. A disagreeable story.

Roxelana has already been observed elevating her son-in-law
Rüstem to the Grand Vizierate over Ibrahim's dead body. She
was even more concerned with the welfare of her own sons, for
one of whom she was determined to secure the succession when
Suleiman should die. She contrived this in the simplest manner—
with grateful Rüstem's collusion, I imagine. No more was necessary than to put it into the sultan's head that his eldest son
Mustafa, already so dangerously popular with the Janissaries, so
strong, so promising as governor of the province to which he
had been sent to learn the art of governing, was plotting to usurp
the throne. Perhaps the rumour was true even. Suleiman believed
it, left the City with a great train and set up his camp at some
distance from his son's provincial headquarters. He then sum-
moned the young man to wait upon him in his tent. It was certainly a tent of great magnificence. Elements of the sort of tent
(though much later in date) can be seen in the Askeri (Military)
Museum: great tent-poles carved in barley-sugar spirals, painted,
gilded, elaborately rich hangings. Into a huge tent of this sort
the young man came, alone, in answer to the summons. He found
it empty. Busbecq tells us that 'lo! upon a sudden, there started
up four mutes, strong and lusty fellows, to be his executioners. . . .
They set upon him with all their strength and might and endeav-
oured to cast a cord about his neck; he defended himself stoutly
for a while (for he was a robust young man), as if he contended
not only for life, but for the empire . . .' This of course is what
Suleiman so feared, as he stood there 'behind a linnen Vail in the
Tent to behold the tragedy; he peep'd out his Head, and gave the
Mutes such a sour and meaning look in reproach of their remiss-
ness' that they redoubled their efforts and soon the Prince Mustafa

was dead. They laid him out on a tapestry in front of the sultan's tent so that the Janissaries might behold the corpse of their 'design'd emperor'. Then the Janissaries turned away 'and silently departed with blubber'd eyes and sad hearts to their tents'; and once there they set to fasting, refusing even water, for days. Suleiman, faced now with their dangerous ill humour, placated them by banishing Rüstem Pasha from office. All this in Busbecq's version, and he does not say how Suleiman placated Rüstem's wife, his own daughter Mihrimah. Roxelana showed no such loss of heart; she went on courageously, to finish tidying up what she had embarked upon. She sent a eunuch to Bursa, where dead Mustafa's little son was living with his mother, and had him strangled. The eunuch had to run for it from the Bursa matrons, who were after him to tear him to pieces.

In this way Roxelana, that good and ambitious mother, made the throne safe for one of her sons. But, alas, she died too soon to enjoy the fruits of good motherhood as Validé-sultane, queen mother, to her son the new sultan. She died in 1553, Suleiman in 1566, when a son of hers succeeded. His name was Selim the Sot. In a short reign devoted to the bottle and the bed there is nevertheless a fine thing to perpetuate his name—the Selimiye Mosque at Edirne, Sinan the Architect's ultimate masterpiece.

Now St Sophia—the masterpiece of the architects Anthemius and Isodorus. A wise visitor will have done some specialized reading to prepare himself for this astonishing building.

Chapter 3

Lunch Hour

THIS is a break with the real business of the day. For food. And I write strictly about restaurant food here, on which package tourism has yet to lay its dead-hand, meat-and-two-veg standards, thank heaven. The City's restaurant menus are standardized nevertheless, but within the tradition the Ottomans spread throughout their empire. Anyone coming here by way of any other east Mediterranean city will attack the food with grateful gusto. It is far superior in what was once the Ottoman capital to food in what were once its provinces and colonies. This is as it should be. As a matter of fact the dishes themselves will hold few real surprises. *Köfte*s are no more than meat-balls after all (though more imaginatively spiced), *kebab*s no more than grilled or roasted meats (the meat less good than the best at home). *Pilaf*s are no longer a novelty to us, however agreeable to find them so good here. Anything 'shish' (*şiş* on the menu) will be anything skewered in English—and lumps of skewered swordfish grilled (usually with a mustardy dressing) are a surprise well worth exposing yourself to. Perhaps the *börek* dishes will be unfamiliar; the flaky pastry we associate with 'sweets' is here often filled with meat or cheese. The *döner kebab* will almost certainly seem strange, but is very good indeed. It is mutton, ideally a boned joint, I believe, but normally in restaurants it will be bits and pieces built up horizontally round a vertical spit to form a solid, densely packed cone of meat, point downwards. In the cheaper places this cone may be quite frankly moulded mince, but whatever the case the spit turns in front of red-hot charcoal (or electric fires so often today) self-basted by its interlayerings of fat and the great cap of fat surmounting it, so that the juices trickle down the sides as cooking proceeds. *Döner kebab* is carved vertically into small thin slices each of which is—should be—well browned and crisp on the outside. It must be eaten hot. A party of two may do well to order first one portion and then the second, sharing each in turn, because anyone eating a portion to himself will never reach the end of it before it has turned cold. Mutton-fat cold.

But apart from baby lamb in the season, a better choice than meat in this part of the world is obviously fish, for generally the meat is indifferent, and the Bosphorus fish, freshly caught, freshly cooked, surely the best in the world. The vegetables too, 'each in its stated season', are excellent, and the cooking and presentation will match the excellence of these materials. None of this is very cheap, but it is cheaper than expensive by international standards. *Raki* is the usual aperitif (some prefer the vodka). The local wines are cheap, drinkable and strictly *vin-de-table*.

You will soon notice that instead of one substantial main dish as the basis of a meal, many Turks taking their lunch-hour break will be busy with what are called *mezé*s—small separate dishes of such things as fish roe salad, egg plant salad, oil-based, oven-cooked dishes such as beans *plaki* served cold, a liver dish, a few *köfte*s, stuffed mussels, vine leaves stuffed with rice, shell-fish and so on in great variety. If an *Iç pilaf* is on the menu try it. The finest rice for it comes from Iran, but whether an Irani rice or an indigenous rice it will be perfectly cooked, with very small currants in it, black and sweet, and sometimes pine kernels. Turks often take yoghourt with rice or meat dishes, a first-class sheep's-milk yoghourt that puts to shame the bottled stuff we are given in the West. As with the *döner kebab* so here again (though for a different reason) two or three people eating together will share a number of these *mezé*s, in this way providing themselves with a much wider and more interesting choice than could any one of them alone at the same price per head. There is a tendency for a Turkish host to feel that ten different *mezé*s constitute a meal twice as honourable as five, and it is of course more lavish to look at; but some of the ten will be mere variants of others, and numbers are not the right measure. There is another tendency that should be discouraged by those brave enough—for the waiter to bring little dishes in addition to your own selection, as if they were personal love-offerings. Of course they are nothing of the kind. Their purpose is to double the bill and the tip, for such offerings are seen to be the most expensive items on the menu—giant prawns, bits of lobster and the like.

If it is autumn, and you are eating in a restaurant at the grandest level, you could order Russian caviar instead of all this, and eat it with a spoon.

In the realms of pastry-cookery the City's tradition will perhaps strike Western palates as over-rich. 'Sweetmeats' sounds the right word for them in English. Odalisk food. They are honeyed, they drip with it, plump with almonds and pistachios, they melt the heart, flopping and wobbling about on the plate, they are absolutely delicious however close to the cloying. Those whose sugar intake is looked after by their wine or *raki* ration will probably stop short of the sweetmeats, and those who watch their waistlines may regretfully stop short too. Yet the *kataïf*s and the *baclava*s and the *loucoum*s and the rest of the harem are not in fact heavy, they are light, like fat girls dancing. Sweetmeats are a possible exception to the City's pre-eminence in the Ottoman cooking tradition. Athens pastry-cooks seem to me to beat the City's pastry-cooks at their own game, and it certainly begs the question. Whose game?

Turks call the City's cooking 'Turkish', Greeks call it 'Greek', the Lebanese call it 'Lebanese' and so on down and round the coast, with regional variations depending upon the materials available. Suleiman the Magnificent would have called it 'Ottoman'.

Would it be right to call it Ottoman? Not strictly speaking perhaps. It is improbable that the Ottoman forbears, a Turki tribe struggling farther and farther west on the long hard trek from their homelands in the high Asian Steppes, could have brought much more of a cooking tradition with them than their cooking-pots—if we except the hunks of raw meat they would pack away under their saddle-bags where the horse's sweat could be relied upon to salt and preserve it. *Pasturma* is the tamed present-day equivalent of this violent stuff. It is on sale in every Turkish provision shop—and in Greek provision shops too. A novice may find it too racy to eat raw, and more acceptable baked with herbs in a greaseproof paper packet.

Is the Turkish cooking of today not Turkish then? Greeks

populated Anatolia and Rumeli [1] for long centuries before the
Ottomans arrived and took the lot. The most sought-after cooks
in the Ottoman nineteenth century, and in earlier centuries too,
I dare say, were Greeks. Is this cooking, then, Greek? It cannot
have come from the Greek mainland in any post-classical period,
anyhow, and there appear to be few, if any, classical references
to cooking except in the most perfunctory sense. The Romans
must have brought their elaborate feeding habits with them to
Greece, but in the long lean vista of centuries after the Romans
left, mainland Greeks must have completely forgotten such
luxuries. Victory in the War of Independence against Turkey
(1821–33) brought rich Greeks from the City to Athens, and
doubtless the City's feeding habits with them, but that does not
answer the question either.

With the Fall of Constantinople in 1453 the Ottomans must
certainly have taken over a good deal of Byzantine cooking along
with so much else Byzantine in flavour, as we shall see; but where
did the Byzantine cooking tradition come from then? Originally
Roman, one supposes, brought by Constantine the Great in
A.D. 324; but it seems more probable that the food the Byzantines
were in due course eating, along with the clothes they were
wearing and the luxuries they were enjoying, came from farther
east, not farther west. The dishes we enjoy today in Istanbul,
where they are not latter-day borrowings from France and Italy,
have a definite Eastern flavour. We may conclude, I think, that
the tradition comes from Iran, Persia. Here it is best sampled at
Abdullah Effendi's ('Mr Abdullah's') restaurant on Istiklal
Caddesi, or at the Liman Lokantasi [2] above the Port Offices; or
at the Konya Lezzet Lokantasi, or Pandelys [2]—a Greek-owned
restaurant that a year or two ago I would certainly have rated
as high as Abdullah's in this short list, but there has been a
serious falling-off in standards lately.

But for lunch today, alas, there is no time to sample the best of
what the City offers. It is 1 p.m., in the heart of the old town, feet

[1] Turkey in Europe of our time—and not to be confused with the Greek
'Roumeli' of Mr Patrick Leigh Fermor's *Travels in Northern Greece*, London,
1966.
[2] Open for lunches only.

are tired, it is hot, and there is a lot more sightseeing to be done
in the vicinity of St Sophia from which you have just emerged.
In any case the traffic has frozen solid as a car park. Eating near
by means eating very modestly; and drinking near by means a
wine-house or a *raki*-bar, and both possibilities are sawdust-
strewn in character if not in fact. In the circumstances the sensible
choice for an old-city lunch within easy reach will be in the Covered
Market (*Kapali Çarsi*), unless since this book went to press someone enterprising has opened a good restaurant somewhere near by
outside the walls, which are not more than a couple of hundred
yards from here, on the Florya Sea Front Road. As it is, everyone
will want to visit the Covered Market anyhow, and lunch hour
today may be thought of as sightseeing rather than good eating.
Those who are to have other opportunities for seeing the Covered
Market may brave the traffic block and struggle off down at a
snail's pace to the Golden Horn again. There they will find
Pandelys (in excellent premises above the 'Egyptian' spice
markets and serving wines, etc.) and the Konya Lezzet Lokantasi
(in less attractive premises opposite the railway terminus at Sirkeci, serving better food but no wine).

Eating-house possibilities in the Covered Market are strictly
down-town, popular and teetotal (except one). At this sort of
place waiters will as a matter of course put strangers at your table
if there is room, or put you at someone else's. If there is no
vacant table you may sit at someone else's with no more ado;
but if you are shy about this, not knowing even the Turkish for
'Do you mind if we . . .?' you must first catch the waiter's eye.
It is rush hour. Rush-hour waiters everywhere are experts at
evasion, so they will successfully evade your eye and leave you
disconsolate. You are not allowed to demand attention with a
shout or a clap or a *ssss*, nor (if at a table) may you clatter the
crockery or bang on a glass with your spoon (one or more of
these expedients being permissible anywhere else in the Mediterranean). I am not saying that service is bad, it is mostly very good
indeed; I am saying that a show of haste or impatience is bad,
even a little shocking, and it may induce in the waiter a certain
nervous reluctance to wait on so boorish a customer. All that is
left to you to do is throw a pitiful look at him as he flies past,

eyes averted, and whisper: '*Bir az bakarmisiniz!*', which means approximately 'Please, a little look at me!'

This is not the sort of restaurant where it would be sensible to order shellfish or even fish at all. You can see some in the refrigerator peering mournfully out at you. The turnover in such semi-luxury food here is too slow for there to be much likelihood that these were caught only yesterday or the day before, or that the boiled prawns were boiled today. The patron will have thought that he must make a showing with a fish or two in one of the finer varieties, and that is all.

There is one rather larger, slightly grander, restaurant in the Covered Market (already hinted at) where wines and spirits are also served. Only the very determined will be able to find it, in a hidden side eddy of the markets. It is called Havazlu Lokanta. The food will not be visibly different from the food in the smaller place, but it will be markedly better, the premises airier and less crowded. There may even be more waiters hanging about than clients sitting down. A strange feature of Istanbul life, this over-staffing. It does not necessarily mean better service, but it certainly gives an air of hospitality. The beer will be iced, the white wine may or may not be chilled, red wine is also available. The really needy may like to do what the down-town topers do—pour a tot of vodka into their beer to enliven it. The brands of wines and spirits here will be the same as in the grand restaurants, because beer, most wines, all spirits, are a government monopoly.

Even the overnight-stop visitors, however, will have time on their one evening to sample more serious food than I have been talking about in the Covered Market—probably at Abdullah Effendi's. Or they can do two highly agreeable things at the same time by going to almost any of the little water-side restaurants up the Bosphorus (avoiding the plushiest and most prosperous looking). There they can sit gazing starry-eyed over the most beautiful waterway in the world and in their mouths a bit of fish to dream about.

Chapter 4

Yesterday and the Day Before

THERE can be nothing haphazard about an empire that lasts the eleven hundred years of Byzantium or the six hundred of the Ottomans. Nor is it just chance that both should have been capable of carrying on for centuries after the virtue began to seep out of them and something else took hold. Not all the magic here is white. Something dark waits around for the weakened and unwary, getting into the brain, knotting it, spiritual counterpart perhaps to the '*nosoi arthritides*' that Gibbon spoke of. It has always been the business of these 'arthritic ills' to knot the City's joints, torture its poor bones. How was the crippling process held in check, even mastered for a brief Indian summer in both empires? What kept them going through the ritual gestures of their lives when in fact it was too late to do anything but die?

In each case the answer seems to lie in the astonishing energy of their springs and high summers—as if they had been internal combustion engines driven by Faith and with a power output far in excess of what was needed. It was as if each empire's administrative system, close-knit, carefully organized, had been an immense flywheel that could store up excess kinetic energy against the long latter days when the motive power would die and nothing would remain but the flywheel and the laws of inertia to keep it spinning, spinning, slower now, much slower, running down, till finally it stopped. . . .

In Byzantium the emperor was the instrument of God's will, backed by this close-knit civil service of his, and by the army his executive. He was both Lord and God on earth, the superhuman unapproachable *basileus autokrator*, symbol of absolute power. Not for nothing does he wear a halo in his mosaic portraits. Yet there were sanctions that set limits to his absolute power. These lay chiefly in the people's established if hardly constitutional right of rebellion. The red buskin might be his alone to wear, but he must toe the line with it. His conduct was regulated by a meticulous protocol. Not an action, not a movement, not an article of clothing even—material, cut, colour, time of day—but was minutely laid down and adhered to, and nobody cared for innovations.

In the sixth century we find the Quaestor Proclus taking a stand against the Emperor Justin I, saying that he would have none of his new ways, 'for I know that in the making of innovations, security cannot be preserved'. In the century following, Mohammed the Prophet of Islam is recorded as having said very much the same. 'The worst things are those which are novelties, every novelty is an innovation, every innovation is an error, every error leads to hell-fire.' [1] Both Byzantine Christians and Ottoman Muslims were to subscribe to this idea till their dying day.

If the Byzantine emperor went too far or not far enough, let him look out for himself. Either the army he was expected to lead into battle, or else the people who required him to hold absolute sway over them in the manner to which they were accustomed, would rise up and overturn him. Where the emperor had not nominated a co-emperor or an heir during his reign (which from early days he was careful to do as a rule), then on his death it was usual for the army to put up a candidate—it could be anyone they liked: birth and origins had nothing to do with it. The Senate and the people would thereupon be asked to acclaim the choice.

But it frequently happened that a usurper with an eye to his own elevation would depose and perhaps assassinate the emperor, or cause this to be done. The usurper would often be a general or a nobleman, or the common enough combination nobleman-general, grown too big; and each time this happened it was the usurper's success or failure that would be evidence of Heaven's own intentions. Once the people had acclaimed him they were satisfied that he ruled them by the divine right they had had it in their power to confer upon him. His word became God, his wars holy and enjoined upon him, world dominion in Christ his ultimate aim. Not for a moment did the emperor or his people

---

[1] *The Emergence of Modern Turkey.* Bernard Lewis, Oxford, 1961. Cited from a separate study by the same authority.

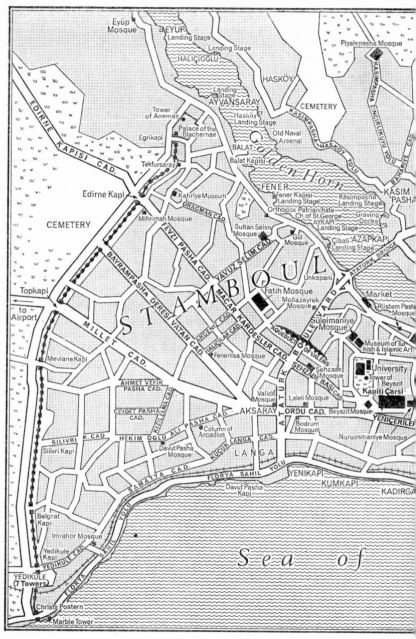

Street plan of Istanbul. (Note: the map is
book. The visitor to Istanbul should

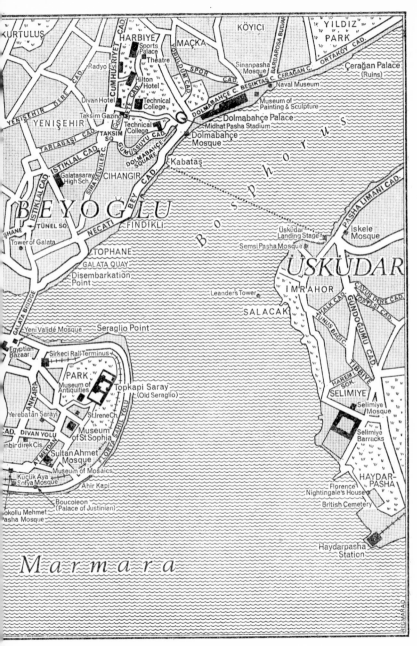

for the reader to use with this particular
arm himself with a detailed tourist map.)

forget that what has been made here below can be as easily un-
made, and it was the ever-present risk of this that brought the
emperor and his civil service to the breaking up of the landed
nobility, the drastic cutting down on army budgets, that weakened
the empire's capacity to defend itself and hastened its end.

It was an age of Faith in God and in themselves. It was also
an age of violence. In recent times we have been readjusting our
attitudes to this; we are now more inclined to say that 'the violence
of the age has been much exaggerated', meaning I expect that we
have talked too often about the blindings and mutilations and
not often enough about the high achievement. The way we invite
ourselves to see it now is that blinding one's son, or cutting off
one's uncles' noses or cutting out one's step-grandmother's
tongue is more clement than killing them outright, and it is true
that time, backed by our changing viewpoint, has somewhat
muffled the cries of all those Byzantine victims, so the splendid
Byzantine hymns to God can now be more easily heard, and their
art (which earlier centuries have ignored or denigrated) can be
marvelled at for what it is and always has been.

Throughout the existence of the Byzantine Empire peace was
seldom long sustained. Moreover the City's enemies were not
like germs, or 'the Bomb', that a citizen becomes aware of only
after they have done him in. Enemies then were four-square and
clearly visible. At good times they were being driven in through
the gates as captives. They would be headed by their kings and
nobles, humbled now and in chains, destined, poor things, for
exhibition in the Hippodrome where a spectacular death had been
thought up for them, and the citizens in their tens of thousands
would be there to watch. In the City's bad times the enemy would
be immediately before the gates, with his war galleys lying out in
the waters of the Marmara biding their time.

We can see for ourselves how Constantine's old triangular
city is two-thirds surrounded by water, and how she rises gently
from her shores as if to display herself to view in her own shop
windows. Anyone can see in from outside, and anyone inside
can see out. In times of siege, which in the Byzantine period
meant very frequently indeed, the citizens need not even bother
to climb the sea walls in order to take a look at the besiegers.

The walls, both sea and land, had always proved impregnable, nor was it gunpowder that in itself rendered them vulnerable at last. A satisfactory method of 'corning' the powder had first to be discovered to prevent the dangerous 'balling-up' that so often resulted in the cannon's bursting in its owner's face instead of expelling an immense cannon-ball capable of knocking holes in fortifications. Reliable 'corning' methods were discovered in about 1420, some thirty-three years before Sultan Mehmet II was to plan his attack on the City, with his newly developed artillery a major element in it. Till this was to come about a long siege might incommode the citizens and bore them, but it probably did not frighten them. God guarded them and they knew it. Food would have been stored up in prodigious quantities, water supplies were assured by enormous cisterns, many of them underground, such as the Binbirdirek ('Thousand and one columns') or the Yerebatan Saray. Moreover until Byzantium's exclusive Greek Fire formula leaked out to the world there was always the comforting reflection that they alone had it.

Just as the people's common law right to rebel safeguarded them against an emperor's excesses or inadequacies, so the constant visual awareness of an enemy, indeed of history's being seen in action under the very eyes, served the emperor as a personal safeguard against his people. Victory underlined his God-given powers; an enemy battering at the gate drove his people to even greater reliance on his capacity to protect them, and one does not change horses in midstream.

But there came a day when they did change horses in midstream, and they lived to rue it. The story is well told by an enemy eye-witness, a knight of the Fourth Crusade that sailed up under the walls of the City in 1203—Geoffroi de Villehardouin.[1] He tells how the people of Constantinople were led into deposing their Emperor Alexius III in favour of his nephew, the Latin nominee, who had fled the City when Alexius had deposed his own brother Isaac, the boy's father. The crusaders now brought back this prince to seize the throne from his uncle. They showed the boy to the people crowding the battlements: 'Here is your rightful

---

[1] *Histoire de la Conquête de Constantinople*, Paris, 1870.

seigneur! For he whom you obey holds you . . . against God and
the Right.' The people fell for it—the boy's youth and good looks,
the magical aura that surrounds a 'prince across the water', the
Return. They deposed Alexius and acclaimed the young man. But
it did not take them long to realize that the young man had sold
them all to Rome, so they rose against him in his turn and killed
him. It was now that the Latins could attack and take the City
with a clear conscience, if such a thing as a conscience were
thought necessary. The City fell to them easily enough. It was the
spring of 1204, and this was to be the most evil day in the City's
long history. The Latins from the barbarous West had never
even dreamed of riches such as awaited them within the City.
Villehardouin could not contain himself: 'Not one of you could
count the cost in gold and silver . . . in vessels. . . . precious stones,
satins. . . . ermine . . . In truth never since the world began has so
much been won in a single City.' Not to speak of women. Villehardouin says that when they broke into the Palace of the Boucoleon down on the sea walls, they found 'the most beautiful women
in the world' all huddled there for safety. Gibbon was to write
of the City's worth in treasure: 'Nor can I better appreciate the
value of that sum in the public and private transactions of the
age than by defining it as seven times the annual revenue of the
Kingdom of England.' Steven Runciman [1] says: 'It is hard to
exaggerate the harm done to European civilization, the books and
works of art preserved from distant centuries were all dispersed
and most destroyed. The Empire, the great bulwark of Christen-
dom, was broken as a power. Its highly centralized organization
was ruined. The conquests of the Ottomans were made possible
by the Crusaders' crimes.'

The Latins held the City for the next half-century and it sank
into the deepest poverty and despair, as if it were some great
house taken over by squatters, the sort that soil the mattresses
and sit around in their own filth.

In 1261 Michael VIII Palaeologus, one of Byzantium's three
contending emperors in exile, retook the City left for dead by the

---

[1] *Byzantine Civilisation*, London, 1933.

fleeing Latins, and it fell to him to rehabilitate it and repopulate it, with the restoration of the crumbling walls a high priority against the risk of Western reprisals. It was now that in his weakness he granted the Genoese a concession in Galata, hoping for Genoese ships to support him in case of need. But when next a fleet was sighted coming up out of the south-west it was Venetian. The year was 1302 and the Emperor Andronicus II reigned in Byzantium, so it was he who must have watched the galleys drawing nearer and nearer. The Venetians attacked the City without success. So they turned their attention to Galata instead, setting fire to it and to their Genoese rivals in trade, with the Byzantines watching the spectacle from their stall seats a hundred yards distant across the Golden Horn. In 1348 the Byzantines were defending themselves from the same stall seats against a Genoese attack; and in 1392 Sultan Beyazit I—'Yildirim' ('the thunderbolt')—arrived to invest the City, unsuccessfully; and this he continued to do on and off for several years. But there were other calls on Ottoman time as well, including Beyazit's great victory over Christian arms at Nicopolis (1396). The year 1402 brought the Ottomans a setback to their rising power, and to the City prolonged respite. Sultan Beyazit was obliged to march against Timurlane, who had invaded Anatolia. Battle was joined in the region of Ankara. Beyazit was defeated and taken prisoner and did not long survive. Timurlane did not choose to pursue his victory, however; instead he turned back from Anatolia for other objectives, leaving Beyazit's sons free to battle for years together over their father's throne, a 'war of succession' that was to colour Ottoman history in a strange way for ever more. The Ottomans did not besiege the City again till 1422. But in 1422 their time was still not ripe.

In the twentieth year of his life and in the second of his reign—in March 1452—the young Sultan Mehmet II set himself to the building of a fortress a few miles north-east of the City on the Rumelian banks of the Bosphorus: Rumeli Hisar ('the Rumeli Fortress') that today provides such a spectacular setting for outdoor summer theatre; *Hamlet, Macbeth, Coriolanus,* produced with tremendous spirit and with the participation of the Turkish Army

D

playing whole companies of Danish, Scottish, Roman men-at-arms. In building Rumeli Hisar, Sultan Mehmet's purpose was to provide a twin to the already existing Anadolu (Anatolian) Hisar across the Bosphorus in Asia, so that the two in combination could close the waterway to all but those the sultan suffered to pass by. 'I form no enterprise against the city,' he told the nervously inquiring emissaries sent by Emperor Constantine XI, 'but the empire of Constantinople is measured by her walls. . . . Have ye power to control my actions on my own ground?'

But the young Mehmet did in fact desire the City for himself above all else, and he spent the winter of 1452–3 in his new-built fortress planning its siege. Then he returned to Edirne where his court was established, there to muster his armies, perfect schemes for employment of his monstrous new cannon and to set the stage for what was to be the City's last appearance in the theatre of war with a production worthy of its greatness.

Constantine XI, the last Palaeologus, knew what was going on—the whole world knew. He had been courting Rome in the hope of Roman aid. Already in the spring of 1453 Ottoman war galleys were nosing round, and the Golden Horn had been closed with the enormous chain to be seen today in the Askeri (Military) Museum. The Emperor Constantine must have been watching from his Palace of Blachernae on the City's land walls, just as his subjects too were surely crowding the walls themselves, watching. An Ottoman host was coming over the skyline from Edirne and encamping on the rolling open ground before the walls, a never-ceasing horde—258,000 men, if the emperor's friend and historian Phrantzes is to be believed. Gibbon believed him; but the figure presumably includes several non-combatants to every fighting man. The City could only muster 'two thousand strangers' under a Genoese general, Giustiniani, and a further '4,970 Romans' to man the walls. With this minute force the City was to withstand fifty-three days of siege.

It is not for me to tell the story of how the City fell. I could not even if I had the space. Read Runciman's *The Fall of Constantinople, 1453*.[1] Of the dawn assault on 29th May he writes with a brilliance

[1] Cambridge, 1965.

that is harrowing to read. It is as if he himself were lost that day five hundred years ago. 'The City is lost!'—and all the bells of all the churches in Constantinople set up their despairing clangour. 'The City is ours!'—and the Janissaries pour in. The last Constantine dies fighting with god-like courage at the walls. St Sophia is filled with citizens paralysed by the recognition of defeat, for there is to be no miraculous eleventh-hour intervention, no promised angel with a sword, no god out of the machine. Instead the enemy batter down the great doors and swarm in on them.

The City was overrun. Slaughter, rape. Then the slaughter and rape gave way to the real business of victory, the plucking of its sweet flowers, the three-days' 'looting' that the sultan had promised his victorious army. For hundreds of years to come still, loot was to be the normal way of rewarding troops for work well done; it is of course the reason why mercenaries fought so well, and why camp followers followed at all.

But in 1453 there was no booty to be found in the City comparable with the booty the Fourth Crusaders had won in 1204, and it must soon have been clear to the victors that the richest available loot was human. They set themselves to rounding up the citizens, dividing them into young and old, chaining them in droves and driving them off to slavery.

An oleograph popular in the alleyways of the City shows Sultan Mehmet as he comes riding in, splendid on his white horse. Noble Byzantine ladies are there, dressed in their finest, offering him bouquets of flowers, welcoming him with smiles (though I do not think it really happened quite that way). By evening of that day the sultan had already turned St Sophia into a mosque and offered up his prayers to Allah there. The night before, the last Constantine had offered up his to God—according to the Latin rite. But the help for which he too had sold the City's birthright to Rome was never to arrive.

From this day on, for 465 years to be precise, till 13th November 1918 (when the victorious Allies occupied the City and triggered off something in the brain of that man of genius, Atatürk), there are to be no invading armies, no investing fleets for the citizens to watch coming up over the horizon, except one, a damp squib, a British squadron come in 1806 to issue an ultimatum it lacked the power to enforce. It had to sail away, somewhat damaged, and with a flea in its ear. But there was to be much else for them to witness within the City as history unfolded itself before them.

By 1453 two hundred and fifty years had already passed since the Ottomans' rough and vigorous forbears had reached Anatolia. The roughness had been sanded down by now. The vigour was still at its peak. But although the earlier sultans had taken, and seemed to settle down in, two Byzantine cities that are accordingly thought of each in turn as the Ottoman capital, both prove in reality to have been little more than staging-posts on the road to Constantinople. It may be that it was at Bursa (taken 1326) and Edirne (Adrianople—taken 1362) that the Ottomans first accustomed themselves to city life, but it was the City itself, the great City, that for long they had planned to live in. They had got it now. It is true that they wore elaborately beautiful brocades (woven at Bursa, an industry inherited from Byzantium) and bore beautifully damascened arms, and their turbans were bejewelled, but these seem to have been just the outward show of majesty. There is nothing to suggest that they had yet succumbed to luxuries in their private lives. But when a taste for luxury begins it is necessarily on a Byzantine pattern, the only contemporary pattern the Ottomans could be familiar with, if not in fact the only contemporary pattern that existed, though itself derived in part from an earlier Persian pattern.

Sultan Mehmet rode into the City with a Persian tag on his lips about spiders spinning their webs and owls hooting amid the vanished glories of the Caesars. He is credited with the knowledge of five languages, one of them Greek. It is not this, however, that proves him to have been a cultivated man. The City's cosmopolitan, polyglot 'Capitulationists' of the nineteenth and early twentieth centuries were far from being cultivated men despite their languages. They enriched nothing but themselves, adding neither a line to the City's poetry nor a page to its literature, nor an inch to its stature, if we ignore the pompous horror of their architecture. The gift of tongues is seen to amount to nothing unless the possessor has something worth saying in them. Sultan

Mehmet had plenty to say and do of the highest order. His capacities and range of knowledge were far wider than could have been needed in a fifteenth-century war lord, even a war lord of genius.

He was violent. An evil temper, it seems. He could be brutal as well as compassionate, in an age of brutality. He is credited with a keen appetite for sex, but in fact is there any evidence that he was a particularly lustful man? It is likely to be true that an insatiable sexual appetite was thought a fitting attribute of every war lord.

By Sultan Mehmet's reign the Ottomans had already developed, at Bursa, an original style of architecture, and very lovely at that. The Ulu Camii (1417) and the Yeşil Camii (1421) are examples of it; and a sixteenth-century reversion to it can be seen in the mosque of Piyalepasha already referred to in the prefatory note as so well worth the time and trouble of even a hurried visitor to the City. Examples of secular architecture of his time can be seen in the celebrated Çinili Kiosk and also in his cannon foundry at Tophane ('cannon foundry') down near the waterfront, a structure that seems to combine the same sort of strength and elegance as the conqueror himself possessed.

He was a patron of the arts, of the Western arts moreover, and this can have been no part of a war lord's popular image, least of all in Islam where, strictly, the representation of the human form is forbidden. But the conqueror had the discernment to invite Gentile Bellini to visit his Court—though his portrait in the London National Gallery formerly catalogued as by this painter is now no more than cagily ascribed to him. Mehmet is known to have wanted Matteo de' Pasti of Verona to paint him too. An imperial page, one Angiolello, who was to write his *Historia Turchesca* based on first-hand experience in Mehmet's saray of the mid fifteenth century, says that Mehmet had Bellini paint many pictures of a 'lascivious nature', but I do not know if any other witness to the truth exists except this ex-imperial page who might only have been concerned to have a dig at his ex-imperial master with a titbit that would help sales without being provably untrue. Angiolello goes on to say that when Mehmet's son came to the throne as Beyazit II (1481–1512) he sold the Bellini pornographs in the bazaars.

The City taken and the dust settled, Sultan Mehmet II pro-
ceeded to assure all Greeks of their safety and of their right to the
free exercise of their religion. He was not only tolerant in such
matters, but indeed actively interested, and would discuss points
of Christian theology with the Greek Gennadius into whose hands
he himself—bizarre situation—was to deliver the crozier of the
Patriarch of Constantinople, following election and investiture
ceremonies carried out with all the traditional Byzantine protocol.
The Patriarch was to take precedence in the State immediately
after the Shaikh-ul-Islam, his Muslim counterpart. The Church
of the Holy Apostles on the Fourth Hill was allotted to the
Patriarchate, but within two years the Greeks were moving out
of it. The Fourth Hill was by now a predominantly Muslim
quarter; it was also exactly where, presently, the sultan planned
to build his Fatih ('Conqueror') mosque in commemoration of
his conquest, and he chose a Greek architect to build it for him.
All this being already in the sultan's mind, perhaps, and known
to be, it was convenient, to say the least, that the Greeks should
of their own accord decide it would be more logical for their
patriarchal church to be set somewhere on the Fifth Hill instead,
where the sultan had settled not only the Greeks remaining (or
returning) after the Fall, but also the much greater number of
mainland Greeks he had imported from the Morea and elsewhere,
to fill population gaps left by death or enslavement or emigration.
Just as he had need of his Genoese across the Golden Horn he
had need too of his Greeks, and he knew it. It should perhaps be
added that a disquieting incident appears to have prodded on the
Greek decision to move: a Muslim corpse had been found lying
across the threshold of the Church of the Holy Apostles, with the
disagreeable implication that the Greeks had been responsible
for the death. The Patriarchate was obliged to move several
times more before coming to rest at St George's in the Phenar
district of the City (Fener on town plans) down by the Golden
Horn, where they are to this day.

In fact Sultan Mehmet the Conqueror was a war lord with a
difference. Even allowing for Bellini's emphasis on the refined
rather than the violent aspects of his sitter's character, we must
admit that the portrait is of a man of great refinement. A copy of

it hangs in the Topkapi Saray Portrait Gallery, and a reproduction in almost any little shop you may walk into in the old city.

For generations already there had been close cultural and social contact between the Byzantines and the Ottomans. At the highest level this is seen in dynastic marriages, such as the marriage of Sultan Orhan (1326–59) with Theodora, daughter of the Emperor John V Palaeologus, whose mother was Anne of Savoy. At a more general level thousands upon thousands of Greek women in Anatolia had presented their Ottoman husbands with sons and daughters. One of John V's sons, Manuel, learnt the arts of war while serving with the Ottoman forces, and where better learn them in the fourteenth century? Manuel in fact distinguished himself under the Ottoman standard. The case of John V's eldest son, Andronicus, was somewhat different; he was living at Sultan Murat I's court at Edirne (Murat had succeeded his father Orhan in 1359), and though this was now a matter rather of 'forced' than willing residence, Andronicus was sufficiently intimate with his great-nephew, the sultan's son, to be in the position to plot with him, quite unsuccessfully, the assassination of their respective fathers. The plot was discovered and the two were blinded by their respective fathers for their pains—rather unsuccessfully in the case of Andronicus, ageing John V proving nervous with the knife.

During the same John's reign the City had been obliged to accept a Muslim community living within the walls, involving a mosque for them to worship in and a Muslim court with Muslim judges. The Byzantines and the Ottomans may not have liked each other—and certainly John V's son who came to the throne as Manuel II kicked out the City's Muslims and revoked their concession as soon as he dared, when Sultan Beyazit 'Yildirim' came to grief at Timurlane's hands; but Byzantine and Ottoman were inevitably linked, love-hate, the ebbing and the flowing tides.

So it need come as no surprise that a scholar such as A. A. Pallis, himself Greek, though his prose style is Eton and Balliol [1] should write that apart from the question of Islam 'the Ottoman

---

[1] London, 1951.

Empire was in many ways a mere continuation of the Byzantine Empire, of which Mehmet II was both the conqueror and the successor'.

The question of Islam is of course fundamental. The Ottoman mind, imbued with it, worked in a manner entirely different from that of the Byzantine mind. But in outward observances the Byzantine ways of life, concepts of majesty, food, clothes, formalities, eunuchs, treatment of envoys, soon also the seclusion of the ruler, all this was taken over. The shutting away of the Ottoman womenfolk is another echo of Byzantium where, in the thirteenth century, the noble ladies lived 'retired and sequestered from the eyes of their fellow citizens'. Even the Byzantine people's right of rebellion creeps in sideways—though there are to be no successful upstarts to usurp the Ottoman throne. There are too many parallels between the two empires for them to be all coincidences or the mere finding of like solutions to like problems; and where bold differences exist they are often exact antitheses, as if one empire were the reverse of the other empire's medal—different aspects of the same thing.

That the Ottomans should later come to such tragic passes was not the outcome of unsound foundations, for the early sultans laid them firm and solid, and by Mehmet the Conqueror's death had developed an administrative system perfectly adjusted to the age and circumstances, very largely due to Mehmet's own great capacities and clear thinking. It was the gradual relaxation of the disciplines on which the system relied that brought the empire low, and specifically—so contemporary Turkish historians agree —a great sultan's withdrawal from the active business of rule, and a weakness in a single aspect of an otherwise vigorous, orderly, sober and successful reign. The reference is, of course, to Suleiman the Magnificent, and to Roxelana his weakness.

Chapter 5

The System (i)

AN OTTOMAN sultan's first and last duty was to prosecute God's holy wars. Muslim lands were 'The House of Islam', the lands of the Infidels 'The House of War', and the Ottoman objective, like that of the Byzantines before them, was world domination in the name of God. The Arabic term for such automatically holy wars is *jehad*. Those taking part in a *jehad* are *ghazi*s. Kemal Atatürk is frequently referred to as *ghazi*, and so is his bridge across the Golden Horn, though it is doubtful if so ardent a secularist ever really thought of himself that way. He was fighting for Turkey, not for God.

These Ottoman wars were not only a holy obligation but also, by divine providence, extremely profitable. Indeed war was the principal source of the early empire's revenues—booty, annual tribute, prisoners to sell off as slaves or else to keep to man the imperial war galleys for the prosecution of further wars, with ransom money quite often a handsome by-product. Sultan Beyazit 'Yildirim's' victory at Nicopolis already referred to (1396), where he decisively defeated a confederate army of 100,000 crusading Christians led by 'the bravest knights of France and Germany', gave into the sultan's hands the young Comte de Nevers, John, son of the Duke of Burgundy and first cousin to the King of France. The youth was taken around on show for a time along with other lesser prisoners before being released against a ransom of 200,000 gold ducats, an absolutely crippling sum for Burgundy to raise.

Wars on an ever-expanding scale required an ever-increasing intake of fighting men. To begin with, the available supply of Ottoman youth had sufficed. They were allotted small holdings to provide them with a peace-time livelihood and must rally to the sultan in times of *jehad*. After a while their numbers proved inadequate to the sultan's needs. Moreover fighting techniques were changing. By the mid fourteenth century the horseman no longer enjoyed the absolute supremacy over the foot soldier that the introduction of the stirrup (from the East) had assured him for hundreds of years together—for it was of course the stirrup that had made mounted shock combat not only so formidable but even possible at all. But with the gradual development of explosives and firearms the sultan must now find infantrymen as well, appropriately equipped; also troops to hold new territories or to garrison new cities falling to his might. These roles—foot soldier, garrison troops—in no sense suited the Ottoman *ghazi* temperament, which was still for the lightning cavalry raid and away, in again to attack and away. Sultan Orhan solved his problem by the enslavement of young Christian prisoners-of-war, converting them to Islam and rigorously indoctrinating them into the Ottoman way of life. With these *yeni çeri* of his, his 'new soldiers' (Janissaries, to the West), he founded an infantry arm that was to be the first standing army in world history. They received no pay at this stage, and were obliged to 'find for themselves' which, as hitherto in war, meant feeding off the lands they took, and rewarding themselves with loot and enslaved citizens for sale. At home, in the intervals of peace, it inevitably must mean 'finding for themselves' at the expense of their own civil population. For the first hundred and fifty years of their existence, however, the Janissaries enjoyed a profitably constant state of war. Their numbers did not then exceed some fourteen thousand. It was Sultan Mehmet the Conqueror who instituted the novelty of paying them a regular wage and providing them with rations, in order to save his subjects from their peace-time depredations. So it was presumably under him that the Janissaries' oath of fidelity came into being. They would swear it on their *ekmek ve tuz*, their bread and their salt.

There was nothing revolutionary about the idea of slave troops. The Abbaside caliphs of Baghdad had for long been kept in power (though in the end kept under) by their Mamelukes, slaves of Circassian origin. Nor were the celibacy and mystic disciplines that Sultan Orhan had imposed on his Janissaries by associating them with the Bektashi dervishes a new idea. Hassan ben Sabbah, the 'Old Man of the Mountains' south of the Caspian at Alamut,

had organized his Assassins on similar lines three hundred years
earlier, and such had been their infamous renown for generations
thereafter that this must certainly have been remembered still and
spoken of in Orhan's day.

Whatever the case, the Janissaries completely fulfilled their
inventor's hopes, at once as fighting men of the first order and in
their absolute, indeed slavish, loyalty to his person. They were
his pride and joy and the terror of his enemies. But recruitment
to their ranks could not keep pace with the demand. For one
thing, by no means every young prisoner-of-war would be suitable material for an *élite* body such as this. By the time Sultan
Murat I was on the throne (1359–89) the need was greater than
ever. He met it with an institution called *devshirmé*. This, in effect,
was a three- to five-year press-gang round-up amongst the Christian youth of Rumelia, Turkey-in-Europe of today. Age: eight
upwards. But with the Ottoman boundaries expanding like bomb-
blast, even this did not long suffice. It was a grand vizier of the
day who saw that whereas not all newly won territories were
profitable accretions in terms of annual tribute, yet lands poor
in gold might yield up rich human material. He reminded his
master that a Muslim sultan's traditional share in all rewards of
war was 5 per cent. Where convenient, let the sultan take his 5
per cent in tribute children for his Janissaries. The sultan was
very happy to agree.

The system was developing. Rules for recruiting officers began
to formulate themselves. Of the new territories coming under
control the most rewarding from the *devshirmé* viewpoint were to
be Serbia, Bosnia, Albania, the Greek mainland, later on Hungary
—all this in addition to Rumelia where it had all started. Strict
standards of selection were to be applied. Only good physical
specimens. An only son exempt, less from compassion, surely,
than with an eye on the same family's capacity to keep going to
raise more sons against a later recruiting drive. Patience has always
been an Ottoman virtue. No Jews. No Gipsies. No Russians.
Strictly no Turks, for the good practical reason that a Turk was
a free man, and a free man, unlike a slave, cannot be obliged to
subject his very soul to a sultan's whim. No orphans, who perhaps
had had to use their wits in order to keep alive.

At the back of all this was the recognition that for a tribute child to serve the Ottoman purpose he must be absolutely unsophisticated, untouched, sound raw material—with 'raw' the operative word, as we shall see. There was also a never faltering conviction that a strong soul cannot exist in a body that is imperfect. So these were the youths and children brought back in convoys every three to five years, the young from whose minds there was nothing to expunge before their new masters got to work on them.

They got to work. First, conversion to Islam. This involved circumcision. The initiatory rite into both Islam and manhood has profound significance for a Muslim. In the City today you will see a Turkish father holding his young son's hand; the boy, perhaps eight or nine years old, wears a decorated sash like an Order diagonally across the chest and a little white pill-box cap with '*Maşallah*' ('as God wills') spangled on it in gold. He walks proudly beside his father, his clothes and his bearing all announcing his circumcision. Some of the most magnificently extravagant imperial Ottoman displays have been to mark the circumcision of the sultan's son and heir.

Once received into Islam in this way, the tribute child was put to the long business of his primary education—Turkish language, Islamic religious instruction, Ottoman ways. In the long years of this first schooling the children were to forget their origins and their families, were to learn to accept fierce disciplines without complaint, monastic privations, hardship. They were to have no protector but the sultan himself, their father surrogate from now on, in his moods benign or tyrannical.

By the time Mehmet the Conqueror came to the throne and the City was his, the Ottomans had already seen that the same *devshirmé* pool of tribute children, providing recruits for the Janissaries, could also serve to provide recruits for other essential services. Everything would depend, however, on the strictest standards of selection. Brought in like cattle from their distant pasture-lands, these poor children would certainly never have believed (even if they had been assured of it) that glittering futures awaited the best amongst them.

As each batch became ready to pass out from the primary

institutions (passionately Muslim, by now, passionately loyal to the sultan their 'father') they would be brought before selection committees organized by, often presided over by, the *Kapi Ağa*, the Agha of the Gate, who was the Chief White Eunuch of the sultan's household. It was as if these youths were being subjected to a series of filterings, sievings, each finer than the last—the stones held back by the coarsest sieve, then the pebbles, the gravel, the sand and so on, channelled off each to an appropriate use. In the scientific selection of personnel there would be little the modern West could teach the Ottomans of four and five hundred years ago.

The first sieving would probably separate off recruits for a corps such as the *baltaci*s (halberdiers). The physical standard would be exacting, the material must be dependable and tough, but it need not be very strong on brain. *Baltaci*s of the 'outer-service' would escort the sultan on ceremonial occasions, indeed most of the various corps would be represented in such processions. A detachment of them, of the 'inner service', would perform duties more or less menial, more or less heavy, in connection with the Harem, and were quartered immediately outside the gate of the Harem by which latter-day odalisks would occasionally emerge for an outing, heavily veiled and guarded by their black eunuchs, to be pushed into the waiting carriages of which you can see examples at Topkapi Saray. Some amongst the *baltaci*s would be supplied with coats having collars that rose high about their cheeks, and artificial locks of hair attached inside to hang like an additional screen to either side. These blinkered 'halberdiers-with-tresses' (*zülflü baltacilar*) would tote the fuel in for the heating of the Harem *hamam*s (steam baths), or charcoal for the *mangal*s, which were—still are—huge braziers of copper or brass that warmed the inmates in the winter, more or less. A double file of scimitared black eunuchs was there to prevent these blinkered, sex-starved men from seeing what they should not.

Another sieving would hold back potential Janissaries. Fine physique, adequate brain. These would be packed off to the Janissary school, a sort of Boys' Battalion, one supposes. The great architect Sinan received his secondary schooling there. That it could equip him to build with such majesty in due course

suggests decent standards of instruction as well as the highest
natural talent in himself. He was a Greek tribute child, born about
1489. He was for years employed on military engineering works,
bridges and the like, in Egypt and elsewhere. It was only late
in his life that he took to building mosques, and he was already
fifty-nine when he built his first great mosque, the Şehzadé (1548),
and eighty in 1569 when he began his real masterpiece, the Selimiye at Edirne (completed 1575). I think we may agree with M.
Albert Gabriel of the French Institute that Sinan was really just
one (the greatest) of a number of directors of public works rather
than architects in the modern sense of the word. They were
members of a corporation, and their marvellous achievements are
the product of their corporate activities.

Where exactly the *bostanci*s come in in the increasingly fine
sievings is not clear, to me at least. These palace guards were
playfully called 'gardeners' (*bostan*—vegetable garden). A special
duty laid upon them was to help with the Harem drownings;
girls tied in sacks, sacks weighted with stones, a little boat behind
a larger boat (for the gardeners on duty), a jerk on the rope, off-
shore there, round Seraglio Point—and over she goes! The gardeners would not even have seen the poor creatures because they
would certainly have been put into their sacks inside the Harem,
probably by the black eunuchs under the supervision of their
chief, the *Kizlar Ağasi* (*kiz*—girl), the Agha of the Girls. The
gardeners would take delivery at the gate of the Harem, and now
for the trudge down to the banks of the Golden Horn, laden with
their bundles. Miss Julia Pardoe, writing her dotty book, *Beauties
of the Bosphorus* [1] speaks of the unlucky girls as 'degenerate beauties
who chanced to offend, to weary, even to disgust the Sardana-
palus of the hour . . .', but thinks, good practical person she
evidently was at heart, 'they would have been better consigned
to the swift currents of the Marmara'. More hygienic, certainly,
than the slow waters of the Golden Horn.

The *bostanci*s seem to have been in the same main cadre as the
Janissaries, but not of them, which may explain one very specific
importance they had for the later sultans: they acted as a useful

[1] London, 1839.

counterweight within the palace walls to the main body of the
Janissaries outside them, whenever the Janissaries cut up rough.
The fact that the *bostanci*s must serve nearer to the sultan's person
than the Janissaries suggests that they would have been sieved
at least with equal care. The *kapici*s (gate-keepers) were another
palace-guard group close to the sultan's person. Closer still perhaps were the palace mutes, whom we have seen performing the
sort of murder that Sultan Suleiman the Magnificent may have
considered outside the range of his official executioners. But the
*sepahi*s (cavalry), the *cebeci*s and the *akinci*s and the storm-trooping
*serdengetci*s ('lost-head' suicide squads in the Japanese manner, I
suppose) and the rest of them can remain, so far as the City is
concerned, just words, instead of different branches of the regular
and irregular armed might of the Ottomans.

We may be content with the *baltaci*s, the *bostanci*s, the *kapici*s
(in their ceremonial Folies Bergère feather headdresses) and the
*peik*s (who wore a costume that seems to have been taken straight
out of old Byzantium), and all of these including the Janissaries
are to be seen in Plate 13—the sultan goes forth on a ceremonial
occasion. Visitors to the Topkapi Saray Portrait Gallery will
find a charming picture on the left-hand wall of the first-room.
It is Sultan Selim III's (1789–1807) annual *baise-main* or hand-
kissing ceremony. He sits just outside the *Bab-i-Saadet* ('Gate
of Felicity') that divides the Second from the Third Court of
the saray. His throne is gem-encrusted gold. It takes to pieces
for campaigning and can be seen in the Treasury of the
saray. The sultan is receiving notables who have come to pay
their respects to him on this auspicious day. He is surrounded by
his various guards. Under the arcade to his right (our left) is a
group of his *iç oğlanlar*—his inner, or student, pages. The various
services we have already briefly touched upon were all recruited
from his *acemi oğlanlar*—his 'raw', or apprentice, pages, the stones,
the pebbles, the gravel, the sand, all these useful substances. But
the end product of the careful sifting is pure gold dust, the *iç
oğlanlar*. For these, whom we may hereafter call pages, quite
simply, there are many more years to come of specialized training
and education. It was for these that Sultan Mehmet II with his
hawk nose and his hawk's eye for the Ottoman advantage was

to build his *Enderun*, or inner-school of imperial pages—some 340 of them, we are told, in his day. There are to be a thousand and more in Suleiman the Magnificent's reign. 'It is not astonishing that the Nation prospers'—as Michel Baudier wrote in his *Histoire Générale du Sérail* in 1624—'since the Turks know so well how to choose the *élite* from great numbers of youths and how to give them the instruction and the discipline which makes them honest men, thus adjusting to the gifts of nature the perfection of art'.

Chapter 6

The System (ii)

SULTAN MEHMET's *Enderun*, the 'inner-school', may well have been destroyed in the great fires at Topkapi Saray in 1664–5 along with much else that Suleiman the Magnificent would have added meantime. It was all built up again and much burnt down again in a succession of fires, of which the gravest were to be in 1856–7. Fire has always been the City's great enemy. But by 1857 Sultan Abdul Mecit had already deserted the saray for his new palace of Dolmabahçe, and Topkapi Saray had become the 'Palace of Tears' in which earlier sultans' surviving concubines were living out lives that now had less meaning than ever. But that is to look ahead.

Over the centuries many travellers have published the little they were able to observe of the *Enderun* and its workings. Only a few foreign visitors were ever able to get beyond the Audience Chamber (*Arz Odasi*) in the Third Court immediately inside the Gate of Felicity, where the Chief White Eunuch had his offices. Some of the imperial pages have left accounts, and of them we have already noted Angiolello's in the fifteenth century and Evliya Çelebi's in the seventeenth. Another seventeenth-century page, a Pole called Bobovi, left also a rough plan of the *Enderun*, drawn not long before the fires of 1664–5, which enables us to identify and place a certain amount even today, where fire spared things or the rebuilding of elements was on the same site. The *Enderun* seems to have existed in a near vacuum, but a little air could get in, a little information leak out. The pages were at least visible from time to time, as in the *baise-main* picture—but this is very late, when things had become slack. Angiolello says that the Grand Turk of his time, who was Sultan Mehmet the Conqueror, 'does not desire that anyone within the palace should converse with the guards who are at the palace gates, or with any other person outside the palace'. And where this sultan expressed his desires we may be sure that the pages were careful to respect them.

Anyone inquiring today about the *Enderun* will find his basic source material already assembled and edited for him in Dr Barnette Miller's *The Palace School of Muhammad the Conqueror*.[1] I lean heavily and gratefully upon her (on others too), but my speculations and inferences must not be imputed to her.

On leaving the primary institutions, the boys thought worthy of entry into the *Enderun* were allocated to one of two junior 'houses'—'Halls', as Dr Miller calls them. The Turkish word is *oda*, which we recognize in 'odalisk'—properly *odalık* with the undotted 'i'—meaning something like 'suitable for the room', and the 'room' would be used for living and eating and sleeping, an all-purpose room in the Ottoman manner. The two junior Halls were the Great and the Small, but were of equal importance.

Working hours would be filled with study of the Islamic humanities. Languages: Turkish, Arabic, Persian. Islamic law (the Shariat). History. Mathematics. Poetry. Music. But at least as much importance and time were given to physical and manual training and, of course, to the arts of war. The teaching staff (non-resident) was drawn from the *Ulema* (the body of Muslim divines) for the appropriate subjects, and from lay scholars for secular subjects. The best poets of the day would be amongst their number, and the best musicians. Robert Liddell,[2] a severe critic, allows himself to say that at its peak the *Enderun* was 'the best school in Europe'.

It has been suggested that once the pages, aged about thirteen by now, had passed in through the Gate of Felicity they were never to catch so much as the sight of a woman till the day of their passing-out, which (for those who made the grade) would be at least seven years later. This is manifestly not true. We know that field sports, archery, horsemanship and other physical activities requiring space for their pursuit would constantly take the pages outside the confines of the palace walls. They must have been constantly seeing women at work in the fields and market gardens, as we still do in the Istanbul of our day. Ottoman

---

[1] Harvard, 1941.   [2] London, 1956.

society segregated the sexes, so that the pages' lack of female company would strike them as perfectly normal, Ottoman-conditioned as they were. This is not to suggest that they did not yearn for a woman; one imagines that much of their time must have been spent yearning—though those exhausting field sports may have taken the edge off it, or have been intended to, as in old-time English public schools. It is to say, however, that in all probability a page would have to wait for his passing out into the world in order to enjoy his first sexual experience of a woman. The really successful page, passing out to some high appointment, might then be aged nearer thirty than twenty, a long time to have been made to wait for his first woman. But on that day he could enjoy her, for the sultan or the queen mother, the Validé Sultane, would have graciously presented him with a number of slave-girls—'odalisks'—as a passing-out prize, along with a suite of pages of his own, and eunuchs and a suitably lavish household.

But passing-out day was a long way ahead, and puberty was at hand, and the processes of nature are very compelling to a youth, so white eunuchs would be in constant attendance out of school. The Great Hall occupied the site immediately to the right of the Gate of Felicity in Bobovi's plan (the Director of the Museum's offices stand there today). It was some 80 feet long and contained fourteen 'stalls', ten students to a stall. It also contained twelves daises slightly raised above the level of the stalls, and on them white eunuchs would sit in pairs. Through the tortured hours of night when the yearnings were hardest to bear, no doubt, these pairs of deprived, envious, invigilating eunuchs would take it in turns to watch for and scotch (if they could) the boys' wretched little makeshift improprieties. Yet, as Ricaut reports: [1] 'In their chambers though watched by their Eunuchs they learn a certain language with the motion of their eyes, their gestures and their fingers, to express their amours'—adding that passions would sometimes boil over in scenes of jealousy. He must be guessing on this last point, but we are obliged to admit

[1] *The Present State of the Ottoman Empire*, etc. Sir Paul Ricaut. London, 1670.

that it sounds a fair guess. We do not know what the eunuchs then did about it.

We know, however, something about the punishments for misdemeanours in general. In ascending order they were scolding, going without food, being 'kept in' while the others were outside engaged in one or other of the violent war games they were encouraged in and so much enjoyed. Then an ascending scale of corporal punishment: light blows on the nape of the neck (a strange place to plant them lightly) with the bastinado in reserve. No one page might be bastinadoed twice in the same day. Very serious offences would merit the amputation of a hand. For theft? This has been a common enough punishment for theft in Islam; but in the *Enderun* an amputation must surely have been accompanied by dismissal from the school, for it could scarcely have served the sultan's interests that a page should have lost a hand.

It was not for misdemeanours only that so vigilant a watch was kept on the pages' days and nights. They were being watched also for the first little sign of disgust at so austere and regimented an existence. Those who were seen to weary of it were seen to have reached the limits of their capacity to profit from their training. But they were being watched above all for evidence of special personal aptitudes and talents—and this was the really important thing. The discovery of unusual talent would determine promotion from the junior Halls to one or other of the specialized senior Halls, according to the nature of the talent. Most of the original junior intake would never get beyond the Great or the Small Hall: they would be sieved out meanwhile and sent to fill vacancies at levels appropriate to their worth in the army or the civil administration. Only those passing the final *Enderun* sievings would be fit to enter a specialist Hall. It has been noted that even such sultans as cared nothing for affairs of state cared greatly about the proper training of their pages, and would sometimes deign to preside in person over the selection committees.

The specialist Halls were four in number. The *Seferli Odasi*— which Dr Miller renders Expeditionary Hall. These pages would accompany the sultan on his journeyings outside the City, whether to the wars or otherwise. They also specialized in music. In fact

Ottoman military music was the nursery for all Western military music, and it can be heard today (but not every day) at the Askeri Museum. It is noisily agreeable, and the old Ottoman uniforms the bandsmen wear give the occasion a special fillip. The *Seferli* pages also had the honourable duty of laundering the sultan's turban cloth to the accompaniment of song. The *Kiler Odasi* was the palace storehouse, the commissariat. Here were kept all manner of imaginative supplies. Great lumps of ambergris sent by the Sultan of the Yemen to his lord; syrups from Cairo; ingredients for the favourite sherbets. Rhinoceros horn and, doubtless, Extract of Lion, almost certainly the useful mandrake root that visitors can still buy today in the Stamboul streets. But as well as aphrodisiacs in plentiful and vigorous supply a sultan would also have need of antidotes for poisons, and they must be on instant call. (The Harem ladies had fairly frequent recourse to them too, I am sure.) The great collection of Chinese celadon ware bowls to be seen in the old saray kitchens (a Sinan building, by the way) were in daily use for the sultan's table because celadon ware was well known to be capable of signifying the presence of poisoned meats in the dish by a slow change of colour.

The *Hasna Odasi* was the Treasury, the sultan's private treasury in which certain of the sultans would themselves periodically deposit treasure. In this case the Chief Treasurer—a white eunuch —and the Sword-Bearer—a page—would together bear up their sultan in a very Byzantine manner. The Chief Treasurer would be under the left armpit (the left being the more honourable position) and the Sword-Bearer under the right—the less honourable position, certainly, but the Sword-Bearer had the advantage of being young, 'entire' and beautiful, indeed chosen for this appointment largely for his beauty.

The fourth specialist Hall, the holy of holies to which presumably all good and ambitious pages would aspire, was the *Has Odasi*—the 'special' Hall. They would be the pick of the pick— the sort of page we have seen receiving passing-out gifts of slave girls. These picked pages would hold high palace appointments and be earmarked for such absolutely key positions in the empire as Grand Vizier, Commander-in-Chief of the Armies, Agha of the

Janissaries and so on. They were in attendance on the sultan's
person.

The relative importance attached to the different Halls is to be
seen in the varying rates of daily allowance granted to their
inmates. Pages of the two junior Halls rated 8 *aqchas* a day. Pages of
the Expeditionary, the Commissariat and Treasury Halls rated 12
aqchas a day, whereas pages of the *Has Odasi*, the special, perhaps
we may say 'private' Hall, in intimate attendance on the sultan,
rated 40 *aqchas* a day. It may be worth recording the allowances
granted to those who were set to train these pages. The white
eunuch 'invigilators' rated 24 *aqchas* a day or thereabouts, and the
lay teachers 10 *aqchas* a day—from which we may see (as Dr
Miller herself points out resignedly) that the teaching profession
was not then better rewarded than it is today.

The Ottoman ideal which this long and gruelling training was
intended to reproduce was the warrior-statesman, the good Muslim, the man of high principles, courteous, quiet, 'gentlemanly'.
He must be of polished speech, which tended to mean a speech
filled with chic Persian borrowings that (Ricaut says) 'fitted [the
speaker] with quaint words and eloquence'. Emphasis was laid
upon silence too, and much upon reverence towards a superior.
The head must be carried low, the hands crossed over the adomen,
a posture that can be seen dozens of times over in the *baise-main*
picture referred to. At all times the behaviour must be modest
and the heart humble. Humility in the old biblical sense was a
quality much esteemed and insisted upon, and it is still marked
among the Turks of today. Coupled with all this, the ideal Ottoman would have tremendous resistance to hardship and privations
(the Turk still has) and he must possess great physical strength.
Weight-carrying among sultans, as also among the City's public
porters, has already been noted with admiration rather than dis-
may.

Etiquette was rigid. Gentlemanly clothes and the eschewing
of effeminate colours. What colours would these be? An example
of each successive sultan's taste in *kaftan*s from the fifteenth
century onwards is on display in Topkapi Saray—and is well
worth examining. Splendid silk brocades with embroidered motifs,
wonderfully preserved, they cover the complete spectral range.

What colours can be left for the ladies to be effeminate in? A fresh pocket handkerchief was *de rigueur* every day. Nose-blowing must be discreetly carried out. Manicure once a week, and it would be unthinkable to have it done in public. (The Palace mutes and dwarfs are thought to have been skilled manicurists.) Once a week the bath, which meant the *hamam*, clouds of steam, scrubbing, being scrubbed, emerging hospital clean, not just superficially soaped and showered. Haircut once a month. No flea-picking in public. (One of the Great Hall stalls was called 'The Stall infested by Fleas' and another 'The Stall infested by Lice'.) The food—as several pages have testified—was awful; but awful or otherwise, it must not be looked at hungrily. However, Knolles, in his *The Generall Historie of the Turks*, etc.[1] tells us that at a saray feast he and his fellow guests were scarcely 'risen up, but certain young men . . . snatcht [the remains] up as their fees and like greedy harpies ravened it down in a moment'. But one hopes these hungry young men were not pages. Busbecq says of Ottoman food of the fifteenth century 'they feed like farmers'—but here again it may well be that the Ottomans fed unwelcome ambassadors and others with food deliberately bad, as we have reason to believe the Byzantines did before them. But to get back to the pages. Onions, never; garlic, never. No belching or hiccoughing at meal times, no yawning or stretching of the limbs at any time. And very important, as a page hastened about his duties, absolutely no 'fancy steps'. No alcohol either.

But we know something about what actually happened, and why the pages were so delighted when they could fall sick enough for admission to the saray hospital, which had wards for each of the various Halls. This hospital was apparently built on the outer wall of the saray, near the *Orta Kapi*, or Middle Gate, that we see today, and to the right of it. Bobovi shows this on his plan. It must have had windows giving on to some relatively secluded corner of the saray grounds, for it was by way of these windows that illicit supplies of wine would be drawn up, brought there by a kindly 'gardener'—for a fee. The penalty, if caught indulging in alcohol, is said to have been three hundred strokes, or else a

---

[1] 5th ed., London, 1638.

three-hundred *aqcha* fine, which would mean twenty-five days'
allowances in the case of a Treasury page. The sultans permitted
themselves this indulgence, naturally, though not all indulged.
A contemporary Turkish historian, Reşad Ekrem Koçu, lists
the drunks among them in his *Topkapi Saray*. They were: Beyazit
'Yildirim', Selim the Sot (of course), Murat IV, Abdul Mecit
and Murat V.

For the reason that a page was in the final issue a slave, and
must be kept in constant awareness of the fact till the day of his
manumission, he might not wear a beard or shave his head, both
marks of the free man. But 'slave' and 'slavery' under the Ottomans (indeed in Islam in general) needs defining. No stigma was
attached to it; a slave was as much a member of his master's
household as his master's own sons. He would be dressed, fed,
treated in much the same manner as anyone else. A slave girl's
son by the sultan was as much the sultan's son (and possibly his
heir) as the son born to him by a wife—in the rare cases where the
sultan married a wife.

This was the System, as we may call it; a slave household owing
allegiance exclusively to the sultan. And these were the *iç oğlanlar*,
the inner pages, who were to go out to rule the empire in the
sultan's name. Their success was a source of constant astonish-
ment and admiration to the West. One Baron Wenceslas Wratis-
law wrote of a diplomatic mission carried out in 1591: 'Never
did I hear it said of any pasha, nor observed in Constantinople
or the whole of Turkey, that any pasha was a natural born Turk;
on the contrary he was kidnapped, captured or Turned Turk.'
One Guillaume Postel said of the Turks in general (before the
second half of the seventeenth century, when feelings began to
change) that 'they felt they were better served thus . . . nor in the
memory of anyone was there a single instance of a Christian thus
nourished who had turned traitor'. Dr Miller has this agreeable
simile, that the Turks were as keen to find and train exceptional
men as Englishmen have been to find and train exceptional horses.
Busbecq says: 'A man's place is marked out by the duties he dis-
charges. . . . Those which at present are the greatest officers under
the Empire were mostly the sons of shepherds and neat-herds.'

He has this to say also, in discussing the Turks as soldiers: 'When I compare the difference between their soldiers and ours, I stand amazed to think what will be the Event, for certainly their soldiers must needs conquer, and ours must needs be vanquished. For on their side there is a mighty, strong and wealthy Empire, great armies, experience in war, a veteran soldiery, a long series of victories, patience in toil, concord, discipline, frugality and vigilance. On our side . . .' And he gives a sorry list of sixteenth-century Western weaknesses, to end with: '. . . and what is worst of all, they are used to conquer, we to be conquered. Can any man doubt, in this case, what the Event will be?' And Ricaut: [1] 'None know so well to govern as those who have learnt to obey.'

So it was 'not astonishing that the Nation prospers'—as Michel Baudier has already been brought in to testify of the early seventeenth century—though in fact the worm was already in the wood and its depredations were very soon to show on the surface too. Nor need it astonish us that the Greeks, scornful of their countrymen and other Christians who had been carried off as prisoners of war or in the *devshirmé* to 'turn Turk' and emerge in time as Ottoman pashas to lord it over them, should have taken over the term *iç oğlan*, inner-page, as *tsoglâni* in demotic Greek, and should use it even today as a term of disparagement.

[1] London, 1670.

Chapter 7

The System (iii)

THE System saw to it that there could never arise an aristocracy of blood outside the direct Osmanli line; nor yet a hereditary governing class—though by the grace of God there did arise a family, of Albanian tribute-child origins, who as the *Köprülü*s served the empire as grand viziers from the mid seventeenth to the early eighteenth century with wisdom and brilliance, and even they could not stop the rot. A feudal gentry did exist on the periphery of things (as in Byzantium). These were the *Derebeys*, the 'border-barons'. At periods they wielded considerable power, but a power always strictly provincial and never a real threat to the City or the sultan's person and throne. It did not occur to anyone that the throne could be occupied by other than a prince in the direct line, so there were to be no upstarts nor yet noblemen generals to usurp it (as in Byzantium). But the System was powerless against another risk, that one of the reigning sultan's brothers should rise against him. The bloody and profitless battles over the succession that followed Sultan Beyazit 'Yildirim's' death were not forgotten. So along with two overriding duties—to produce a son and heir and to wage the very profitable Wars of God—a third duty was bound upon a fifteenth-century sultan on accession: the killing off of all his brothers. It was thought quite correct, therefore, when that highly civilized monarch, Sultan Mehmet the Conqueror, had his small half-brother killed—strangled, in the proper manner. One does not shed imperial blood. It was in fact the Conqueror who legalized fratricide where the throne was concerned. Bernard Lewis, whose *Emergence of Modern Turkey* [1] may be thought of as required reading, quotes this sultan's edict on the subject of fratricide in another work—*Istanbul and the Civilisation of the*

[1] London, 1961.

Ottoman Empire.[1] It goes: 'To whichever of my sons the Sultanate may be vouchsafed it is proper for him to put his brothers to death, to preserve the order of the world. Most of the *Ulema* allow this. Let them therefore act accordingly.' We have seen the *Ulema* teaching Islamic theology to the *Enderun* pages; we now see them, or 'most of them', seeking Koranic sanction for the sultan's edict, and finding it easily enough in a verse which says: 'Discord is worse than killing.' Sultan Mehmet III (1595–1603) had to kill off seventeen of his brothers on his accession. Many of the little things were still at the breast (being the product of many different mothers) and there is no reason to believe that Mehmet's grief was simulated as he followed the procession of seventeen biers to the tomb that stands in the southern forecourt of St Sophia— a small tomb, like an appendix to the larger one. He killed his own son at the same time, together with the boy's mother, because the latter had gone to a soothsayer for a charm that would enable her child to succeed to the throne at an early date, so there was in fact an eighteenth bier in the procession. The mother did not rate an imperial tomb.

Sultan Ahmet I (1603–17) was to modify the fratricidal law. He came to the throne at the age of thirteen; the next of kin was his brother Mustafa, who was weak in the head. Sultan Ahmet spared the mad boy's life, but kept him incarcerated in the saray. A foolish precedent to have established. From this reign on to the end of the eighteenth century we are to have the astonishing spectacle not only of the sultans' brothers being incarcerated for life in the saray, but of the sultans' sons being incarcerated too, from about the age of five. Gone the days when the son and heir would learn the business of rule by being sent to govern a province under some wise ex-page (as murdered Mustafa, son of Suleiman, had done); they were now just simply immobilized for life. They were not mistreated; they were provided with lodgings decent enough, no doubt, though not luxurious, except for the heir's apartments, which are rather fine. (Those who visit the Harem— closed at present for extensive works—will see these apartments. They will be described as '*Şehzadelar ve Veliahd Dairesi*', and they

[1] Oklahoma, 1963.

antedate Sultan Ahmet's edict of course.) The imprisoned princes were provided with barren women for their solace as soon as they were of an age to need solace; and if by ill luck a woman conceived it was easy to get rid of mother and child. The princes were richly clothed, I dare say, though fed 'like farmers'. It is untrue to say that once in they would never again see the sun or the moon in the sky; in fact they lived in a great walled-in area, deep as a well—and if the heir-apparent's apartments were given to the boy, then he had an airy terrace, marble-paved, with a wonderful view of the Golden Horn. This terrace is described on the official museum plan of the Harem as *Kafés Tasliği*, and over-looks not only the outside world but also the walled-in area referred to above. The whole closely guarded area was called the *Kafés*, which can mean anything from lattice, or grille over a window, to a cage. 'Cage' seems the fittest rendering here. Only the son or brother (as it might be) nominated as successor on the death of a sovereign would ever come out of the *Kafés* again alive. The saintly Sultan Suleiman II (1687–91) had spent thirty-nine years in the Cage, busy and happy copying Korans, before he emerged for a reign he did not enjoy at all. He loved only God and longed to go back into the Cage to carry on copying out His word as revealed to the Prophet, but instead he died of a dropsy outside it. Sultan Osman III (1754–7) had spent fifty years inside before emerging for his brief and uneventful reign in which his most interesting achievement was the edict that suddenly obliged women to wear the veil.

We can now see that the sultan was safe from 'border-barons', from upstart usurpers, from a governing class, from his brothers and from his sons. We can also see that the Cage was not a very good preparation for the man or boy destined to ascend the throne. And in the next chapter we shall see who the sultan's enemies are to be.

Chapter 8

The Beginning of the End

THE Ottoman Empire starts with a succession of ten sultans bold or brilliant, sometimes both, and (as we have seen) Turkish historians today date the beginning of the empire's end from the middle of the tenth reign, that of Suleiman the Magnificent, whom the Turks call 'The Lawgiver' (1520–66). By this time Byzantine concepts of majesty have been completely taken over, though modified to suit the Ottoman temperament. Luxury was by now an integral part of pomp, silence was thought to be in keeping with the almost holy aura surrounding sultans, much as mosaic haloes had hovered above Byzantine emperors' heads. When Suleiman's father conquered Egypt he assumed, and passed on to his successors, the Caliphate of Islam; he had become Commander of the Faithful and Shadow of God on Earth, as his Byzantine predecessors had been His vice-regents here below in their time.

White eunuchs as officials of the court on the Byzantine pattern had already come in by the time the City fell to the conqueror; black eunuchs were to follow, for harem duties, as the seclusion of women became more and more the thing. Black eunuchs must have been comfortably installed at the Eski Saray ('old palace') on the Third Hill at the time when Roxelana was making the first of her two known (or at least reported) strategic withholdings of her person from the sultan's person. She had come off a sorry loser in a hair-tugging, face-scratching set-to with a Harem rival, Bosfor, mother of Suleiman's first-born Mustafa (for all the good that was to do poor Bosfor). Roxelana thereupon quite simply declined to answer any summons to the sultan's bed till time should have restored her damaged beauty. She is said to have been small, russet-haired, lively, and her Harem name—

Hurrem—meant something like 'lively'. We call her Roxelana for her Russian slave-girl origins.

Suleiman the Magnificent was the first sultan to withdraw himself from his grand viziers' councils in the divan chamber at Topkapi Saray—the *kubbealti* ('under the dome'). It was more majestic now for him to remain concealed behind a grille high in the back wall of the chamber. No one could ever be sure if the Presence was there or not. It was significant too that access to the little room behind the grille, to the listening-post, as it were, was through the Harem, which was closed to all except the sultan, his women and the black eunuchs.

Sultan Suleiman had had his war-lord triumphs of course: Belgrade in 1521; Rhodes in 1522; Buda, and soon after it Pest, in 1526; Azerbaijan in 1535; Tunis too in 1535—and in the same year the great corsair Barbarossa (a Greek 'turned-Turk' as Haireddin) personally took Algiers and presented it to the sultan. Failure of Ottoman might before the walls of Vienna in 1529 was scarcely a triumph and was probably talked of less.

Suleiman's withdrawal of himself into his *selamlik* (or personal apartments) and his Harem seems in effect to have been like the gradual withdrawal of the motive force that had always driven the Ottoman machine. The laws of inertia were to keep the great flywheel spinning for generations yet; there were enormous reserves of kinetic energy to draw upon; but there was to come a time when nothing was being put back and the empire began to slip and slither in a collapse at first almost imperceptible. There were to be moments when a sultan on the old warrior-statesman pattern would set the engine working furiously again. The boy Osman II might have proved such a one if he had been allowed to live. The rowdy, roistering, bloody, drunken, debauching, victorious Sultan Murat IV, who was dead of his excesses before he was thirty, was certainly another. Selim III at the end of the eighteenth century and Mahmut II in the first part of the nineteenth were good men and of high principle. But by then it was far too late for reform. The whole thing had collapsed inside.

The first signs of degeneration were already clear for Suleiman the Magnificent to see, but did he see them? Perhaps he believed too implicitly in the omnipotence and infallibility ascribed to

him. Like the Byzantines before him he had a fine contempt for
the West (modified in the case of France) and was blind to Western
progress till the West had already outstripped him. He may still
have been for us the Grand Turk, but for all his reputation in the
West he is seen to have been weaker than his womenfolk. First
it was his mother, a slave in his father's Harem, Hafiza. Roxelana
was to follow. She was already doing extremely well in the 1520s,
with the birth of several imperial children to her credit. This was
to secure her manumission, but it was well before motherhood
that she had accumulated riches enough to bring on the access
of piety that nothing could assuage but that she build and endow
mosques to the glory of God. We are here obliged to remind
ourselves that such pious acts enriched the donor's heirs in perpetuity, the setting up of religious trusts being the only certain
means of securing one's fortunes against a sultan's greed. But
Roxelana, that poor distracted pious beauty, was only a slave.
Slaves were not permitted to endow mosques—what a laughable
idea! So she had to wait till she bore her lord children and was
in consequence manumitted. And then all at once she must have
been struck by a hideous recognition: her piety and sense of
honour must henceforth compel her to withhold herself from the
sultan (for the second time) because it would be very disgraceful
for a free women to yield herself to him—unless of course the
sultan chose to marry her. 'Which he, doting for love, would do'
(so Busbecq writes) 'against the custom of the princes.' To the
utter consternation of his subjects Suleiman married her. With
Roxelana's face-scratching rival well outdistanced, with the
sultan's mother dead (in 1533), Roxelana was supreme—once
the other woman's first-born Mustafa had been got rid of as
already described.

So in the end there is really no need for Roxelana to tie up vast
fortunes in the endowment of mosques, because the greedy
sultan who is going to covet it will be first her own son, then his
son, and so on in perpetuity. At least I suppose this is how her
orderly mind must have worked, since she does not seem to have
endowed a mosque at all.

I do not know at what date a great fire at the old palace (where
Suleiman's Harem was still housed) gave Roxelana the pretext

for a triumph of a different kind. She managed to prevail upon the sultan to let her move from the burnt-out ruins of the old Harem to Topkapi Saray with her immense personal suite of slave girls and black eunuchs. In this way she ensured that her days as well as her nights might be spent close beside him.

When Roxelana died, and although no other woman ever seems to have taken her place in the sultan's ageing heart, it cannot be said that Suleiman was at long last a free agent. There were always the Janissaries that his predecessors had controlled brutally but effectively, but of whom Rüstem Pasha, the son-in-law Grand Vizier, had said to Busbecq years earlier: 'You know', said he, 'it is a time of war whereby *they* may be said to reign rather than the sultan himself, who stands in fear of them.' It was Suleiman himself who had granted some of 'them' the right to marry. We are entitled to assert that this concession was wrung from weakness; Suleiman could not have been stupid enough to offer it like a bonus. Two reigns later the concession bears its inevitable fruit; Sultan Murat III, that hopeless misfit, is acceding to the Janissaries' demand that their sons be enrolled in the corps. This is thought to have been in 1582. By 1592 the majority of the Janissaries was made up of sons of Janissaries, second-generation Ottomans. There is no doubt that to be a Janissary was highly profitable; free native-born Ottomans must have been deeply envious of the converted Christians' monopoly in these rich pickings. And in consequence by 1594 we hear of Ottoman Turks being admitted to the Janissaries' ranks. In the saray itself the same sort of softening of the disciplines is evident: by Sultan Ahmet I's time (1603–17) there are cases of Turks 'enslaving' brother Turks to offer to the sultan as presents, in the confident expectation that the 'slave' thus offered would one day be in the position to reward his benefactor. A Grand Vizier under this sultan, one Mehmet Pasha, was a free-born Turk 'enslaved' in this fashion. By the time mad Mustafa was momentarily on the throne (1617–18), the Janissaries had the power to kick him off it and back into the Cage from which his nephew emerged to rule as Sultan Osman II at the age of fourteen. Osman did not have long to wait before the danger was clear to him. Campaigning in Bessarabia two years later he was forced to abandon the 'siege

15. Istanbul University. The date (1453) is the date of the death of Constantinople and the birth of Istanbul. The university was not founded till the nineteenth century.

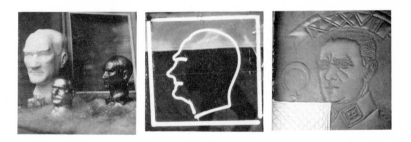

16. Atatürk lives on—statues, portraits, photographs, metal plaques, or as here, in busts (marble, brass, bronze), neon lighting and even quilting.

17. *Art-nouveau* ironwork daisies to be seen on Istiklal Caddesi
(*page 101*).

18. Girls on Ataköy Beach.▷

19. Girls in a cookery class.▷

21. Taxi-*dolmuş*—stuffed
full of people, as a *dolma*
is stuffed with rice and
currants. Each of the eight
passengers pays his fixed
share (*page 8*).

20. Istiklal Caddesi—the new city's most popular
thoroughfare—shops, theatres, cinemas, 'striptiz'
—'a nineteenth-century canyon, too narrow for
its function ... (*page 101*).

22. Beyoğlu, the newcomer's first impression, a spiritual lodging-house land, till the buildings part and the city's 'three seas', Marmara, Bosphorus and Golden Horn, lie shining down below.

25. Village *güreş* (Turkish
wrestling). 'If you can
only get it right . . .
your oily enemy . . .
must stay long minutes
ignominiously up-
ended . . .'

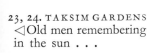

23, 24. TAKSIM GARDENS
◁ Old men remembering
in the sun . . .

Young man forgetting . . .
▷

26. Hero, heroine and villain.

of the fortress of Khotin because his Janissaries were treating with the enemy'.[1] Once back in the City, Osman determined to lay plans for their extermination; he would slip away on the pretext of some pilgrimage, raise an army and return to do the job once and for all. But his plans became known. So the Janissaries took him and dragged him to the castle of Yedikule, the 'Seven Towers' against the City's land walls, and there killed him most brutally. The clothes he was wearing that day are on exhibition at Topkapi Saray, torn and bloodstained. So mad Mustafa was brought out of the Cage a second time to continue his little interrupted reign. But he was no good, of course, and they soon took a bowstring to him.

Whereas the palace guards, the *bostancis*, had a regimental vocabulary based on 'gardening', the Janissary vocabulary derived from the kitchen and the idea of 'food', starting with the oath of allegiance on their bread and salt. A Janissary in the ranks had a wooden spoon stuck in a socket in the front of his headdress as if it were a *panache*. The cauldrons in which their soup was made were to become objects of veneration to them. Before setting out on campaign they would pile these cauldrons, soup-kettles, before the tent of their commanding officer, their *orbaci*, or soup-man. A Bektashi dervish would bless the kettles solemnly. Food, its acceptance or its refusal, was to become the means of signifying their temper, rather as a child will gobble up its porridge to please its mother, or refuse it in order to defy her. Each Friday a detachment of Janissaries would parade for a meal to be publicly eaten in the Second Court of the saray. The sultan would be present. The order would be given for the *pilaf* to be brought— a rice dish rather than soup, it appears, on these ritual occasions. If at this the Janissaries' only move was to reverse their soup-kettles, it meant they refused to eat; and this meant something seriously wrong. It was most often complaints about arrears of pay, short measure in the rations or the cloth issues, sometimes about the admixture of false coin in the money they were paid with. Charles White in his *Three Years in Constantinople, or the Domestic Manners of the Turks in 1844*[2] says that 'where the sultan

---

[1] A. A. Pallis. London, 1951.   [2] London, 1846.

was powerful enough and if the complaints were exaggerated, a short silence would ensue'—and then the Chief Executioner would appear with a strong escort of *bostancis* and *baltacis*, and in no time at all the ringleaders amongst the Janissaries would be no more and their heads would be on display outside the *Orta Kapi*, the Middle Gate, and the executioner would be washing up a bit at the wall fountain near by, which is called, for this reason, 'The Executioner's Fountain'.

But often enough it was the Janissaries who won the day and would demand a victim, such as the Chief Black Eunuch, eunuchs being their traditional enemy. Any scapegoat. He would be promptly strangled and his body tossed out to the waiting Janissaries, who would string it up on a tree in front of their barracks.

Now the Janissaries can throw themselves in ecstasy upon their food and adore again the sultan their father, as he adores them too, at present, for is he not an honorary private in their ranks, their own comrade-in-arms, just as the great Maréchal Lyautey was an honorary corporal in the French Foreign Legion and their companion-in-arms? Plate 14 shows two Janissary officers, a 'soup-man' and a 'chief water-carrier'. It is a photograph of one of the mannequin groups, life-size, to be seen in the Askeri Museum. They wear authentic uniforms from the early nineteenth century.[1] The faces, painted wood, and the postures of this group and the others show the eager wolfish look that must have been thought proper to these devilish creatures who could depose sultans for no better reason than to secure the traditional 'donative' from the new sultan, a sum they saw to it should increase with each successive reign; who could enlist whole companies of fictitious 'recruits' and thereafter themselves draw the additional pay and rations; who could (and did) beat up and rob private citizens with impunity. They 'got' the first of two reforming sultans, Selim III (1789–1807); but the second reformer, Mahmut II, 'got' them instead. In June 1826 Mahmut II finally felt himself ready to take the action he had been planning for so long and with such care. In the City alone, not to speak of the fortresses

[1] Since writing this, new groups of figures totally lacking in distinction have been set up. The old nineteenth-century figures are still on view, however, but hidden away in corners.

outside it and the distant garrisons, he cornered not less than five thousand and perhaps as many as nine thousand of them and massacred the lot. This was at the At Meydan, once the Hippo-drome, where one day in A.D. 532 the Byzantine general, Beli-sarius, had cornered tens of thousands of the rioting Green Circus faction, closed the gates on them, and slaughtered his lot too, with systematic efficiency.

The massacre and dissolution of the Janissaries is to Turkish historians of today 'The Auspicious Event'. A comfortable phrase.

Chapter 9

The Monstrous Regiment of Women

THOUGH *Kadinlar Sultanati* is the exact translation of the 'regiment of women' that Calvinist Knox declared to be so 'monstrous', there is a distinction. What horrified Knox was that a woman should reign at all, whether Mary of Scotland (at whom he blew his 'First Blast of the Trumpet') or any other woman. We notice, however, that when shortly after this Elizabeth I of England came to the throne he blew no second blast at her.

The idea that the daughters as well as the sons of the great and powerful should be given appropriate educations was already solidly (though only temporarily) established by the time Elizabeth was born. So she read Greek and Latin, spoke French and Spanish, could play upon the virginals and, when the time came for it, compose and deliver speeches of Churchillian eloquence. She was cultivated in much the same way as Sultan Mehmet II had been a hundred or so years earlier, and she proved to be as well equipped as he was for the great role she too had to play.

What was 'monstrous' about the Ottoman 'regiment of women' was quite simply that the women in question were monsters—narrow, ignorant, unscrupulous, self-seeking—yet in a position of supreme power. 'All power corrupts and absolute power corrupts absolutely.' Of course they only became practising monsters when the weakness of a sultan enabled them to use their power. Till then they must be mice; but the Harem was a very different cageful of mice from the *Enderun* with its imperial pages that the walls of the Third Court divided from them. A page could come to power and glory only by first giving proof of his

74

worth over years of close observation—ample time to test his honesty and the nature of his talents and indeed to develop them. This is to say that the *Enderun* pages had to be exceptional human beings as well as handsome and of outstanding physique, whereas the girls bought for the sultan's bed need only be young, beautiful and submissive. And so they were—on the day they arrived. But the little odalisk who has it in her to succeed must be quicker off the mark than need be a page, before the magnolia-petal charm she hopes will prove sexually irresistible to her lord starts getting brown at the edges.

Recruitment for the Harem was mostly from the public slave markets, which drew their supplies from the spoils of war, captives of corsairs or of the Ottomans' own war galleys, and so on; but in fact many of the girls thought to be the most desirable were not captives at all but willing products of what were virtually slave farms in Circassia and Georgia. Children, either kidnapped or otherwise acquired from their parents, were collected together with a specific end in view—that some rich house, and the richer the better, would buy them. Circassian and Georgian serfs would often bring up their own children in a like manner, for sale. Topkapi Saray, the richest house in the world, must have been hung before these little girls' eyes like a bedtime-story melon of a moon to cry for.

The City's slave-girl business was very much in the hands of 'middle-women', who would have access to the great Harems. A man buying in the market for his own household would have the right then and there to see the girl's face, her 'breast' (both?), her arms and her legs (though not above the knees); but once he had approved her in this general fashion, and a price had been provisionally named, he was allowed to have the girl pass a night or two in his Harem, where amongst other things her sleep would be carefully observed—did she walk in it, snore, grind her teeth, or sleep perhaps more soundly and unrousably than would befit a slave? Also had she any discernibly 'filthy habits'? (Charles White's phrase) [1]. One must suppose that the prospective buyer would sleep with her if he was buying her for the bed and not for

[1] London, 1846.

hard labour, and assuming that she were not being sold as a
virgin, subject to a midwife's medical examination. But virgins
would surely never be sent out on approval.

Some men would want virgins for their beds, others would
prefer training and accomplishments. The Chief Black Eunuch
of the sultan's household would know what would best suit his
master; it would presumably depend upon the imperial person's
own degree of sexual experience. Certainly no one would ask it
of a corsair's captive that she be a virgin when she came ashore,
even if this had been her condition when taken aboard; and
possibly one of the great attractions of the Circassian slave farm
product would be a combination of virginity plus a trained
capacity to please. Observers have recorded that the little Circassians and Georgians 'readily thrust out their tongues . . . and
submitted to other scrutiny' in the open market. I suppose they
knew (or at least believed) what the corsairs' captives did not—
that at last they were on the royal road to honours and enjoyment.

If the *Enderun*-school is to be thought of as a near vacuum,
then the sultan's Harem was hermetically sealed. N. M. Penzer's
The Harem [1] partially unseals it, and his book is the fullest single
work concerning it in English that I know of, though he in his
turn leant heavily upon Dr Barnette Miller's earlier study,
Beyond the Sublime Porte. [2] Few outsiders, being male, ever got in,
and for those few it was no more than a brisk run-through when
the sultan was absent, at the wars, perhaps, or away hunting, or
staying at Edirne. Clandestine visits were occasionally arranged
by a friendly or venal *bostanci* with the co-operation of a senior
black eunuch. The only male outsider I have read of who ever
claimed to have seen any of the girls themselves was a certain
Dallam—English—come in 1599 to install a marvellously elaborate organ set about with mechanical blackbirds and such. He had
built it at Queen Elizabeth's command, as a present from her to
Sultan Mehmet III; and as Dallam alone knew how to assemble
this complicated thing the Harem doors were obliged to open for
him. Passing before a grille inside, he caught sight of a group of
girls playing in a garden beyond it. He stopped to stare, excited

---

[1] A new issue: Spring Books, London, 1966.   [2] Harvard, 1931.

by their beauty and particularly by their thighs, which were visible through the fine lawn of their 'britchis'. But his escort hustled him on angrily, and it seems that later he had to run for it when four black eunuchs appeared, brandishing scimitars.

With the Harem taking over from the *selamlik*, the white eunuchs have already had the best of their day. The black eunuchs are now to have theirs, and it is to keep fine for them for centuries —for such of them, at least, as survived not only the cruel trek across African deserts, chained, driven like oxen, but also the trifling surgical intervention that was to fit them for their new calling. The operation was often performed en route, in mid desert, with nothing but hot sand as a styptic to cauterize the wound. Mortality was high. Those operated upon before puberty were seen to stand a better chance of survival; and also, in their case, the prostate would atrophy or something of the kind, and they were never to suffer the torment of desires they could not satisfy. White eunuchs for extramural work (Circassians and Georgians preferred, as with girls for the bed) would normally lose only their testicles. The black Harem-eunuchs lost the penis as well, just in case of miracles, and as an additional precaution hideous physical specimens would be deliberately chosen as a rule against the possibility that, denatured though they were, they might still arouse desire in the hearts of the neglected, frustrated, sex-starved women they were required to guard. For if the *baltacis* were sex-starved palace guards of a sort, the odalisks were sex-starved too—for they were to be numbered in their hundreds, and there was but one man available to them, their lord the sultan. Not all these women, surely, could learn to accept (and fewer still would actually enjoy) the lesbian relationships that are known to have been commonplace, and inevitably so. The black eunuchs nevertheless are thought to have helped the ladies out in other ways, and, after the invention of rubber, they would obligingly smuggle in dildoes. We cannot know that they tried them on, but I expect they did, and eagerly.

These, then, were the attributes that enabled a black eunuch's importer to demand for him three or four times the price of a white eunuch in the slave markets of seventeenth-century Istanbul.

But not every black eunuch can hope to be bought into the
sultan's Harem, and, of those who are, only one at a time can
become Agha of the Girls, with a guarantee of immense power
and wealth—which he will salt away, in Egypt as a rule, against
the need of instant flight. Too often, alas, flight was not instant
enough, as we know from the stories of Janissary risings. Other
occupational risks and disadvantages seem to have been weak
eyes, poor memories, incontinent bladders. They had little silver
quills tucked into a fold of their toppling turbans; these were
convenient for urinating through; and if this was a tiresomely
frequent necessity, yet it had its good side too, because a eunuch's
urine, by some process of unsympathetic-sounding magic, was
much prized as a specific that would overcome impotence in
entire men. So perhaps the Agha of the Girls could sell his, along
with preferment and other favours. Alcohol meant little to the
eunuchs as a rule. Sweets they loved. And music.

Eunuchs may have lacked the physical strength of entire men,
but their emasculation did not make cowards of them. Far from
it. They were, for example, champions at a murderous game called
Cerit in which teams of horsemen would gallop about hurling
wooden javelins at the opposing side. Sultan Mahmut II (1808–
1839)—the reformer—was to ban this game. This infuriated the
black eunuchs because here, at least, was a field of activity in
which they could demonstrate their physical superiority over
the real men they envied. At archery too they excelled; and at
intrigue of course. A *Kizlar Ağasi* is seen in Plate 13. He rides
third in procession, immediately behind the sultan's Sword-
Bearer, whose place is immediately behind the sultan. This particular 'Agha of the Girls' looks fairly normal; most were
obscenely bloated—whereas white eunuchs were apt to be pear-
shaped, with old, old women's faces. Leila Hanoum, a courtier
of the second half of the nineteenth century, speaks of Harem
eunuchs in her book *Le Harem Impérial et les Sultanes au Dix-
Neuvième*.[1] 'These debonnair creatures', she calls them (I translate
from her son's French translation of her Turkish text), 'who live on
excellent terms with both women and men, with never a thought

[1] Paris, 1925.

to cross a soul unless one should trespass on their preserves
—then, and only then, they become ferocious.' Leila Hanoum's
book is fascinating for reasons that would surprise her: it
is the courtier, gossip-columnist, side-aisle view of an impossible
institution that she most loyally believed in and upheld. Indeed
she probably did see it all as splendid, and all princesses (the
'*sultanes*' of her title, sultans' sisters) as beautiful.

Certainly all the girls chosen for the sultan's bed throughout
the centuries must have been considered beautiful, but for a girl
to be received into the Harem was no more guarantee of success
than for a page to be received into the *Enderun* school of the golden
period. It was only a beginning, and, for girls recruited not for
the bed but for rough work (strong girls; Negro girls were fairly
general for this purpose), it was the end rather than a beginning.
For the 'beauties' it was essential to get 'noticed', and this was
not always so easy. Life and behaviour in the Harem were strictly
protocolaire. Ottoman social segregation of the two sexes being
what it was, the sultan would ordinarily come visiting from his
selamlik only for one of two reasons—to sleep with a girl, who
had been apprised of his intentions, or to visit his mother, the
Validé. He would never be alone while in the Harem, one
imagines, so that even if he had wished to he could not relax the
convention that he give no public hint of his sexual desires and
preferences of the moment, though the libertines Murat III,
Mehmet III and Ibrahim may well have behaved very differently.
I have come across no evidence to suggest that the sultan held
inspection parades, for example, though it is likely that the Chief
Black Eunuch would see that his own favourites among the
girls got 'noticed' and that those he disliked did not. Probably
the only times when all the girls would be gathered together
in one place (I am thinking of the Topkapi Saray Harem, not those
at Dolmabahçe or other nineteenth-century imperial Harems)
would be for some fête day gala, or for a musical evening in the
Hünkar Odasi ('Royal Salon'), the one room in the Harem large
enough for receptions of the sort. It has a minstrels' gallery where
the *Enderun* pages' orchestra would sometimes be brought in to
play, tightly blindfold. This room has been ascribed to the architect Sinan, and if this is so may we perhaps guess that Suleiman

the Magnificent commissioned it for Roxelana? But it has been terribly mutilated since their day by wanton decorators.

So I suppose it was in the *Hünkar Odasi* that the girls could best hope to see their sultan and get seen by him. But a girl, no matter how beautiful, would be two or three hundred times less notice-able and diminished in her beauty if she had to be just one of that number of others as beautiful as she was. Miracles could happen, or pieces of pure luck: 'they' say that an imperial handkerchief would sometimes get laid on someone's shoulder as the sultan passed by—but a favourite of Sultan Mustafa II's (1695–1703) told Lady Mary Wortley Montagu that the story of summons by handkerchief was absolutely untrue. And indeed if the convention of secrecy in such matters is true, then the handkerchief story is probably not.

The place above all others where a girl would not only see the sultan at close quarters, but stand an excellent chance of being seen by him, was undoubtedly the Validé's apartments, where the sultan would sit with his mother sipping sherbet or coffee, an intimate scene. It would be part of an imperial mother's love for her son to keep a lynx eye open for the least little signal he might give her, a covert glance at the junior coffee-maker, for instance, a pensive look away. Nothing might be said, it seems; everything was extremely decorous; but the girl in question would know and mother would know. Not for nothing had she learnt in her own youth that sex is the most important weapon in the world. The girl is now *gözde*—'in the eye', the sultan's eye—and that is what every girl in the great rambling Harem is after. It will be for the Validé to set the wheels discreetly moving, through her Controller of the Household or else the Chief Black Eunuch, as soon as her son has respectfully taken his leave of her.

Lucky the girl who gets *gözde*. She is taken and bathed and perfumed, on go the depilatories if there seems even the remotest need of them. Her hair is dressed, often in tresses down the back with ropes of pearls plaited in, she is arrayed in borrowed finery, hung about with borrowed jewels carefully inventoried by the Lady Keeper of the Jewels, no doubt she is in a state of consider-able emotion—'pray God let me conceive!' Slowly, elaborately, violently, the *maquillage* goes on with a trowel, very violent in colour too we are told. As in the candle-lit capitals farther west, no fard less violent than violent red or chalkest white will be visible at all at night. Eyebrows, if Nature has not already joined them in a 'bow' (the eyelashes were thought of as the feathering of arrows—a simile from the Ottoman snob sport, archery), will at certain periods be joined now with thick black paint—and over in the Third Court at these periods the *Enderun* pages will be painting theirs in too, though who for, heaven knows. In the Ottoman Empire, as in the Byzantine, a natural junction of the eyebrows has been a point of beauty. It is fairly common today with men: but Turkish women perhaps separate theirs in the interests of a more international vogue. Highly perfumed, violently coloured, the odalisk is set apart in a room to herself, with attendants. Her coming good fortune is an absolute secret that everybody in the Harem surely knows and nobody mentions, and a great many people bitterly resent.

But after all this preparation and excitement the summons sometimes does not come; the sultan was not serious, as men ogling girls in buses or pinching their behinds if they get half a chance are not always quite serious. Or else, again, the Validé misread the sign language, though Sultan Ibrahim's desires were never in the slightest doubt I am sure: he once asked for—and got—the fattest woman in his whole great City. She was a smasher. Armenian. But of course Ibrahim rode rough-shod over polite conventions.

So when the summons does not come the stood-up *gözde*-girl is soon stripped of her borrowed finery; and her rivals, I fear, are noisily exultant over the failure that puts the poor girl back where she belongs, with them, on her pallet in a cold damp dormitory, stone walls, stone floor. Nowhere can be colder, damper, than the Topkapi Saray Harem. Going in once, a quiet autumn day, sunny and beautiful outside, a Topkapi Saray official said to me: 'Just a moment, I've forgotten my overcoat.'

But on some luckier night, for some luckier girl, the longed-for summons comes. She is conducted in reverent silence through the hush, finger to lips, white eyeballs of black eunuchs rolling unctuously under the wobble of the moving candlelight—to the chamber where the imperial lover is already laid out in a great bed under a baldachin. Is the chamber dark? I imagine so, rather dark. Does he greet her? I doubt it; he is likely to pretend to be unaware of her presence even; this would be the more lordly part, and over-eagerness quite wrong. But she has been carefully briefed about the etiquette, how she must approach the foot of the great bed with awe, lift the border of the coverlet, lay it first to her forehead and then to her lips in a sort of obeisance, and then, watched by, encouraged, even prodded on by, a couple of 'old Moorish women' attendants ('Moorish' certainly means African, and these two are said to have sat around all night there) she will go through the tricky business of slipping in under the bedclothes without too much disturbing them. The bedclothes are not tucked in, so it is less difficult for her than it would be for us, yet it cannot have been all that easy to wriggle in under them, past the sultan's waiting feet, nor to manage with any grace the 'upward glide' that is to bring her to her 'resting-place' beside her lord. I do not know if anybody knows for sure today whether the sultan lay naked under the bedclothes, or whether the odalisk herself at some point in the proceedings must gracefully slip out of her own finery, or most of it. Perhaps part of the old Moorish women attendants' duty lay in receiving items of clothing as they were gracefully passed out under the coverlet—but I am speculating here, of course, and speculating also (on the basis of what we know about the generally prudish character of the Ottomans) as to whether perhaps both participants went through the motions fully clad and clanking with jewellery.

So that was that. In the morning the triumphant girl will get a present and some money and the sultan will leave behind as one of her perks the clothing he has worn, though this may possibly refer to no more than a sanctified night-shirt—but whatever it was she would want it. She could probably sell it for a fortune. Did she leave before him? I think she must have left first; and in that case she would have to trust the old Moorish women to let her have the night-shirt later, because her sultan lover would still be in it. In any case a wise girl would be leaving a nice fat tip out of her takings in gratitude for the faithful watch the old women have kept all night. She may have need of their good offices again, if she is lucky enough to get another go.

The next move on and up for the luckiest of the *gözde*-girls
would be admission to the charmed circle of the *ikbal*s. This word
in modern Turkish means 'success' or 'good fortune'. In the
nineteenth century the sultan would limit himself to twelve such,
but the number may well have varied from reign to reign. They
seem to have represented within the Harem what the pages in
personal attendance on the sultan represented in the *selamlik*.
*Ikbal*s were in attendance within the Harem, as pages—and since
of all the girls available these twelve had been chosen by the sultan
because they corresponded most closely to his tastes in such
matters, these are the girls with the most chances of conceiving
an imperial infant.

A girl giving birth to a male child ('Oh! let it be a male child!')
might then be elevated to the coveted rank of *kadin*, of which (as
with wives among ordinary Muslim mortals) a sultan might have
four, numbered one to four now, their names no longer used. To
be a *kadin* was to be the equivalent of a mistress with a nice solid
irrevocable settlement, safe, no matter what befell, provided
she behaved. Often they would be married off later to some
pasha or other. It is wrong to call these *kadin*s '*sultanes*', for the
latter title was reserved for women of imperial blood. A *kadin*'s
daughter by the sultan would rate the title, assuming she were
allowed to survive. She would then use it as a suffix, thus—
Mihrimah *Sultane*—though in fact the 'e' is a Frenchification
for the feminine gender: Turkish makes no such distinction. If
'Mihrimah *Sultane*' had a child in her turn by her pasha husband
someone would forget to tie the umbilical cord or be guilty of
some other little carelessness which would result in the infant's
death.

A *kadin* must be extremely watchful of the other *kadin*s. Each
would have her separate apartment within the Harem and her
own suite of attendants, but all are in it for the same thing, to be
the mother of the next sultan. The higher the mortality among the
other *kadin*s' male babies, the better someone else's chances. So
mortality was high here too, and the *kadin*s would guard over their
infant sons with the utmost vigilance and have the food served
only in Chinese celadon-ware bowls, I dare say, till the day the
boys were taken away for ever and put into the Cage for the rest

of their lives or came out to ascend the throne—whichever earlier.

These are the *gözde*s, the *ikbal*s and the *kadin*s—counted in tens. But for the majority of the several hundred girls and women in the sultan's Harem, life is not going to be a success story. On the contrary, both life and love are to pass them by, except for seven or eight of their number who will one day become the powerful lieutenants of the all-powerful Valíde, the queen mother. Life, if not love, will reward these few; each will preside over an *oda*, attended by her odalisks. They will be the Lady-Controller of the Household, the Lady-Treasurer, the Mistress of the Robes, Keeper of the Jewels, of the Baths, of the Store-House and so on, with the Head Nurse and the Head Laundress and the rest, all the way down the scale (Plate 8.) All will answer to the Valídé and discipline will be as strict as in the strictest days of the *Enderun*; and although life sounds on paper to have been lavish (we know that it was) the courts and corridors and chambers in which it all took place are really just as poky and disappointing as, say, Holyrood Palace. The Valídé's private apartments are an exception to this: she had a suite of three rooms on two levels, with a delightful view over tree tops to the Golden Horn from one of them. But they are quite ungrand, and will not become grand merely by furnishing them sumptuously. Various of the sultans had apartments named for them on the boundaries of the Harem proper. Some are moderately grand, one or two charming, none (obviously enough) grand enough to suit the rocketing fancies of an Abdul Mecit, sultan between 1839 and 1861, who caused an Armenian to plan him a Dolmabahçe Palace, which must be seen to be believed.

But back in the Harem still, the *kadin*s' apartments, and those of a sultan's unmarried sisters, would be one- or two-roomed affairs, sometimes an improvised duplex with an interior ladder-like stair up to a little low-ceilinged gallery over the built-in clothes closets. In some cases a lavatory like a bathing-hut stands outside, equipped with a marble squat, and sanitary conduits festoon about the corridors like the trunks of masonry trees.

When current researches are complete and published, and cur-rent restorations of the Harem itself are finished and the Harem opens its doors to the public, decorated, furnished, relit, it will be very different, and we shall know much more than the little we can at present piece together and speculate about. But meanwhile, if we did not even know that little about it and what it represents in terms of life and blood and death, it would have no power to hold our attention for longer than it takes to glance in, shiver, and go out back into the sunshine again.

1603. The tradition of Harem rule is well established by this time. Already seventy years have passed since Roxelana gained her ascendancy over Suleiman and lost it only by predeceasing him. Her successors do not make the same mistake. Nur Banu takes over, first as *kadin* to Roxelana's son, Selim the Sot, then as queen mother to her own son by Selim, Sultan Murat III. But with Nur Banu's death there is someone waiting to take over even more powerful and determined, ruling first her lord the Sultan Murat III and, with his death, their son, Sultan Mehmet III, who left her a completely free hand both in and out of the Harem, being himself exclusively concerned with sex. It is 'Safiye' ('blonde') Baffo, a Venetian of this now extinct noble house, captured by a Turkish sea captain and either given or sold to the sultan's Harem as a slave. 'Safiye' is constantly listening in at the 'listening-post' above the Divan Chamber, constantly interfering in politics and is an immense power in the land. She made only one mistake—from her point of view: she succumbed to her assassins, the black eunuchs of a Harem faction that dared to attack her, Safiye-Validé, on her own ground and got away with it.

Now for the greatest of them all, a woman far outstripping her predecessors—the indomitable, ruthless, extraordinary *Machpeiker*, 'Moonface', better known to history as Kössem.

It is believed that she was the daughter of a Greek priest. She was to rule from the secrecy of the Harem for fifty years, or nearly, starting off as the mother of Sultan Ahmet I's first born in 1604. Ahmet was fourteen that year, a boy father. How old was Kössem? She is to die in 1651, and it is generally thought that she was then at least eighty. Even if she were nearer seventy than eighty at her death (to make allowance for exaggeration of the legendary old

woman's age) this would still make her in her middle twenties
or so to Ahmet's thirteen, when first they brought her to his bed.
Her maturity, together with the undoubted strength of her will
and her personality, may well have assured her ascendancy over
this weakling from the very start. Ahmet is to be lost to us after
his deposition in 1617, put away into the Cage he had instituted
for his brother Mustafa as an alternative to the bowstring.
Kössem is not lost to us. We shall be witnesses of her death when
her time comes, and she does not die easily. But meanwhile she
is to show the world how infinitely more splendid it is to be the
Validé than to be any boy-sultan's favourite. Let him have a hundred girls, a thousand to choose from (Murat III had more than
a thousand, we are told), help him find them, put them in his
way. Sultan Ibrahim's sexual capacities astonished all, including
his mother Kössem, I dare say, and he once drowned the entire
contents of his Harem, having got bored with the same old faces,
three hundred-odd of them: into the Bosphorus with them—
why not? Plenty more where they came from, the slave markets
are full of them, his imperial pockets are full of gold (so are someone else's), plenty more where that came from too. But a sultan's
mother is different, she is unique; there is only one of her and her
name is *Machpeiker*, 'Moon-face', Kössem Validé, and she is to
outlive five sultans and threaten to get the better of a sixth. Of
these five we have already dealt with the father of her children,
Ahmet I. Next comes Ahmet's brother—Mustafa. Mad. He is not
allowed to last long before being deposed. Back he goes into the
Cage to make way for three of Kössem's sons in succession (we
can ignore Mustafa's momentary return to the throne in 1622,
and note merely that he gets the bowstring this time). Two of
her three sons succeed as minors: Osman at the age of fourteen,
slaughtered by the Janissaries at eighteen. No heir. Next Murat
IV, who accedes at thirteen and at twenty-nine dies childless of
his chosen excesses, which include drink but not women. Now
comes the Ibrahim already referred to, the third of her sons to
succeed. He is a debauchee, which from the Validé's point of view
is almost as good as being a minor—he won't interfere; but when
Ibrahim gets the bowstring in his turn in 1649, he leaves a little
son to succeed him—Mehmet, aged six. Mehmet has a mother,

Harem name Tor Han. Kössem has of course foreseen this disagreeable situation and plotted ahead of events. She has another
son waiting in the Cage, in reserve as it were: Suleiman, no longer
young by now, presumably. If she can get Suleiman put on the
throne instead of little Mehmet, then she, Kössem, can remain
Validé. Apart from the intoxication of power, it is worth remaining Validé. A Validé of no special consequence in the 1840s is
known to have had an income the equivalent of £110,000 a year—
say around $300,000. What can we multiply by to arrive at the
buying power today? And by how much more to arrive at the
income of the greatest, greediest, most ruthless validé of all time,
Kössem, with the empire still nearly at the peak of its immense
wealth? Kössem intrigued desperately, using the Agha of the
Janissaries as her ally in the outside world. Suleiman's claim to
the sultanate must be admitted.

But she fails. Ibrahim's little son accedes. Tor Han, the mother,
becomes Validé. Kössem refuses to leave the Harem. Tor Han's
position must be intolerable—but she has to put up with it, for
a year, a second year, though not in silence. Kössem has the Agha
of the Janissaries as her ally outside. Tor Han has the Grand
Vizier; she also has most of the *Enderun* pages (they have become
monsters of intrigue themselves by now) and within the Harem
the reigning Validé's traditional ally, the *Kizlar Ağasi*, the Chief
Black Eunuch. Kössem has the support of the Commander of the
bostancis, in the Second Court of Topkapi Saray; and in the Third
Court, the sultan's Sword-Bearer. In the Harem itself she can
still control many of the lesser black eunuchs. I do not know how
the odalisks sided on that day in 1651 when it is all to happen.

Tor Han knows what she is up against—the only way out for
her is to encompass Kössem's death; and to this end she very
correctly secures a *fetva* (edict) from the Grand Mufti authorizing
Kössem's execution. Kössem, whose business it is to be at all
times well informed, hears of this and sends frantic word to the
Agha of the Janissaries to take the appropriate action. Accordingly he goes at once with a body of his Janissaries (it is night)
to surprise the Grand Vizier and give him the ultimatum—
Kössem's son Suleiman on the throne in the place of Mehmet.
The Grand Vizier plays a trick: he asks leave to go at once to the

G

saray in order to convene the Divan; but no sooner is he inside
the great gates of the saray than he has them slammed behind him.
A minute's breathing space.

Everything goes very quickly now. The Grand Vizier has Tor
Han roused in haste; oaths of allegiance to the child sultan Mehmet
are sworn all round, the Grand Vizier draws up a decree for the
boy to sign, on the authority of the Grand Mufti's *fetva*—his
grandmother, Kössem, is to die.

We cannot know exactly how it happened. Tor Han's Harem
ally, the Chief Black Eunuch, must have awakened her. Others
would waken too: Tor Han's apartments were certainly full of
sleeping attendants. There is the presage of murder in the air,
murder quickly, before the Janissaries can batter their way in
and the general slaughter starts and it is all too late—panic com-
municates itself, it can be felt like a presence, the air is thick with
noise and commotion, and of course Kössem knows. Somehow
she sends a message to her ally in the Second Court, the Commander of the *bostanci*s. Quick! Open one of the small side gates
of the saray and let the Janissaries in! But her enemies are already
coming for her, the Chief Black Eunuch and his underlings, so
many of them, and she is suddenly alone. Who is going to overdo
the courage and the acts of loyalty when everything is already
lost, and seen to be? She hides in a clothes closet. Which room
would it be? I don't know. They drag her out, this poor terrible
old woman whom everyone has abandoned, they pull her, scream-
ing surely, kicking, scratching, hysterical, out across the court-
yard of the Validé sultane, and into the dog-leg of the vestibule
leading to the Court of the Black Eunuchs (*Karağalar Tasliği*)—
and as they drag her they tear her clothes off her, grab at her
jewels (they have already taken the gold she flung at them as
earnest of more to come, much more)—out through an arched
exit called the Gate of the Aviary. But she must be dead by now.
And her naked old body, battered and broken, is thrown into the
silence of the Third Court.

They had finished her off, strangled her, as if this were necessary,
with a cord that hitherto had only held back the curtains of her
bed: and a curtain it is that should come down now to hide the
anticlimax of a barrow in due course, or possibly just a sack and

someone's shoulder, perhaps a *bostanci*'s, with a limp old cadaver slung over it.

The Ottoman Regiment of Women really began in earnest the day that Selim the Sot's Grand Vizier, Sokullu Mehmet Pasha, was assassinated. This great man was a Bosnian 'turned-Turk' and so long as he was in power all went smoothly enough on the surface; but with his death it starts to show, the disintegration of everything the Ottomans had so carefully built up. Fortunately for the City, and for us, Sokullu Mehmet Pasha's lovely mosque was finished (1571) before the assassins got him. I personally think this the architect Sinan's most beautiful—as opposed to most splendid—piece of work in the City.

Kössem is the last woman to rule from the Harem. A renaissance begins a few years later with the appointment in 1656 of a new great man as Grand Vizier. Was Tor Han Validé wise in this, or just lucky? Did she know what she was doing when she accepted his terms on behalf of her child? His terms were 'absolute power in his hands alone'. Von Hammer, the historian, calls him 'vice-emperor' rather than 'first minister'. The man was Mehmet Köprülü, of Albanian extraction—as already related. He was succeeded by five other Köprülüs, one after the other, though to be accurate one of them, Karamustafa Pasha, was a connection rather than a close relative. It was the Mustafa Köprülü serving under Suleiman II at the end of the seventeenth century who said that 'all the successors of Soliman the Magnificent had been fools or tyrants, and that it was time to abolish the race'.[1]

[1] Gibbon quoting Marsigli's *Stato Militare del' Imperio Ottomanno*, 1732. (Everyman edition, vol. vi, page 343.)

Chapter 10

Today

THE great Atatürk could defy the Allies and their Treaty of Sèvres and get away with it, he could depose sultans, abolish dynasties, he could bring into being a new authentically Turkish State, set aside the Islamic *Shariat* in favour of civil and penal codes based on the Swiss and the Italian; he could force the Hat on to peoples' heads in place of the Fez they had grown attached to in the hundred years or so since Sultan Mahmut II had introduced it to their reluctant forbears. He could have abolished the veil for women too, but in fact, knowing that most of his country-women would feel naked and disgraced without it, he did no more than actively discountenance it. He could and did abolish the dervish fraternities whose woolly metaphysics so benumbed the simple (including foreign visitors). He could change the hours of the day and night, and the months of the year, and reject at last the beautiful Arabic script that was so hopelessly unsuited to the Turkish tongue—e.g. the same combination of Arabic letters لو ل و was obliged to do service for two Turkish words of absolutely dissimilar meaning: *ulu* (great) and *ölü* (dead). In short he could alter the flow of events from 1922 onwards, and cause his country's past chronicles to be rewritten by Turks as history, with entirely new emphases. One thing he could not do: invent and set in motion a complete new Turkish way of life. Ways of life do not spring fully armed from anybody's head, as Athena did from Zeus's. Not even from the head of an Atatürk.

In the City of today the duties the citizens discharge earn them enormously disparate rewards. Social stratification is by income groups, not the blueness of blood; but the Joneses are just as busy keeping up with the Joneses as anywhere else in the world, each group aping the ways of the group next richer, in the old familiar fashion. Poor, middling, affluent, rich. And just as the Ottoman sultans necessarily took over Byzantine patterns of grandeur and luxury, so the older rich here continue to live in opulent-looking seclusion according to patterns necessarily based on the Ottoman hangover. A glance into the antique shops gives the key: ornament, elaboration, encrusted surfaces, over-stuffing, a sort of Jumbo Louis-Quinze-cum-Philippe'ishness and the bigger the better. Queen Victoria was right to give the sultan the largest chandelier in the world to hang above a carpet the size of a tennis court in his new Dolmabahçe Palace. This taste for size also goes for enormous examples of objects essentially small, say pearls or diamonds. The Treasury at Topkapi Saray is the place to see some—huge and sleepy and bored-looking in their isolation.

The younger rich seem to follow a trend more 'contemporary', in the glossy-magazine sense, more American; but the middle-grade furniture shops show that the Joneses still coming up are still to be wooed with Baby-Jumbo reproductions of the Dolma-bahçe ideal. The very poor are unconcerned with 'taste', being too poor for such luxuries, too poor even to have Joneses to keep up with; but if there is no money for them, there is always the euphoria of *keyif* plus the Turkish capacity to resist cold, heat, hunger, thirst, pain and the awful cruelties of life. They have something else that must somehow see them through—resignation, and their true humility. Suicide, if not unknown, is rare. The official *Annuaire Statistique* gives figures for forensic examinations of the living and the dead, the woundings and the drownings and the strangulations and all manner of things both sudden and ghoulish, though surprisingly few of each. There is no column for suicide.

All classes, including the classless poor, appear to subscribe to the old Ottoman 'gentlemanly' ideal, and it is agreeable for everyone that most people should be courteous and quietly good-mannered and considerate to each other and to strangers in public (which means us). The Turk is still the 'Gentleman of Europe'. One of them, a particularly cultivated man, said to me in his perfect English: 'A Turk is nearly always a gentleman. But Turk*s* . . .'—he emphasized the 's' of the plural—'well, that may be different.' I asked him what he meant exactly, but he became vaguer instead of more explicit. I think the following is true, at least—that if the sum total of Englishness generated by ten Englishmen is, say, twelve or thirteen times the Englishness of one of their number, then we must step up the sum total of Turkishness generated by ten Turks to twenty, thirty, I don't know how many times more than that of one of them. Turks seem to be as agglutinative as their language with its huddle of suffixes, propinquity, the physical need for it, elbow anonymously in your ribs, men holding hands, embracing—which tittering foreigners (though only the most stupid) have interpreted as evidence of some guilty sexual relationship, whereas it is a clear refutation of any such thing, just a guileless means of communication. So that when Turks are moved by a common emotion, Turks in the plural, they can change like the gears of a car, up to 'overdrive'. Is it this, plus courage and endurance, that makes one Turkish regiment rate two (we remember Korea, after all)? And on a day in 1956, Graeco-Turkish relations over Cyprus being at their worst, and with a rumour flying around that the Greeks were planning to destroy the house far away in Greece that Atatürk was born in, is it this that brought the City into sudden, solid intimate awareness of its national identity? There were fears that the Patriarchate might be the focal point for demonstrations, and the Chief of Police ordered it to be strongly protected. Nothing happened there, but people will tell you that the streets elsewhere were filled with a common purpose, Turkish flags were suddenly waving outside shops in token of loyalty, but with gaps; and where there were gaps, shop windows were smashed, doors battered down, and then the hooligans took over and the looting began, while the bridges over the Golden Horn were hastily opened like fire-breaks. The City awoke next day to a strange silence.

'Knowledge'—anybody's—has always been revered here. A phrase such as the following from Islamic scriptures would be engraved above the entrance to a *medresseh* (Islamic school): 'Whoever taught me a single word, I am his slave.' But in 1839, so Geoffrey Lewis tells us,[1] 'the only educated body of men was

[1] London, 1955.

the Ulema, who saw no reason for change'. There has been profound change since then. Knowledge is revered not only in others today, but feverishly sought after. It may not be Islamic jurisprudence that is the popular goal, but it is still Law nevertheless. In recent years the University of Istanbul's Faculty of Law has counted nearly nine thousand students, of which two thousand-odd were girls. The faculty next in popularity has been Science, counting some five thousand (of which one thousand were girls)—this of a total student body numbering twenty-six thousand plus.

Schooling today is no longer the prerogative of the rich and well-sponsored. It is free, and primary education compulsory. Promising students can win State bursaries that provide for them (modestly) both in and out of the classrooms, and in return they must undertake to serve in some State department for a set number of years after graduating. Alas, there is still a disablingly serious lack of teachers (they don't want to 'guide' or interpret for us either; they want to be lawyers, scientists, engineers). Standards cannot be high enough when classes of sixty or seventy are common and must often be fitted into a double-shift system, one shift out in the playing-fields while the other is in the classroom, with the same harassed teacher to do duty for both. There are no comprehensive schools as yet, and no system I am aware of for weeding out the unteachable, though here we may remember the brilliantly exact system of sieving out the *Enderun* pages. Apart from State institutions there are private institutions such as the Robert College on the Bosphorus at Bebek (an American foundation, 1853). It has done admirable work, the standards have been as high as in any university in the Eastern Mediterranean. Instruction is in English (except for such subjects as Turkish History, etc.). It has always to date been excellently staffed, is wonderfully housed and equipped—and expensive, naturally. Only the sons, and daughters, of the well-to-do can benefit.

The elaborate census returns each five years showed in 1965 that nearly a third of the City's population was still illiterate, but the determination to stamp out illiteracy and improve standards of education does reap an increasing crop of adequately educated citizens. Moreover there is a secondary crop of great significance:

the slow but progressive desegregation of the sexes, to which co-education is surely one of the prime contributors. Of course there have long been groups of artists and intellectuals among whom no such segregating barriers exist, but in a general sense it was not this *avant garde* who broke down the first barriers. It was music, Western music at that, and sponsored by the sultan. I owe this unexpected fact to Bey Faruk Yener, a highly musicianly citizen. He told me how in 1719 Sultan Ahmet III's ambassador to Paris sent back an excited dispatch to the effect that he had just witnessed a strange and exceedingly expensive entertainment —theatre, ballet, song all in one. Grand Opera. Results were slow in coming about: Selim III some eighty years later was the first sultan to see such a performance for himself—indeed all to himself, and his court, in his palace. But by the 1840s Donizetti's *Belisario* and *Lucrezia Borgia* were both being given public performances (visiting Italian companies)—the choice of opera doubtless determined by the fact that Donizetti's brother then directed the Palace Symphony Orchestra. Ottomans were already looking westward musically by this time, and their Turkish successors have never looked back—except at the level of the *gazino* ('casino'—cabaret). Turks are the only eastern Mediterranean Muslims so orientated, and today they can boast, and do, of internationally first-class singers and instrumentalists, artists such as Layla Gencer (soprano), Ayhan Baran (bass), Orhan Günek (lately of the Scala, Milan). Idil Biret, a young woman in her mid twenties, is a pianist of the most brilliant order; another woman, slightly her senior, Ayla Erduran, is a violinist of equal reputation.

Grand Opera blazed a trail that soon theatre on Western lines was to follow, though the shadow theatre, *Kara Göz* ('Black Eye' —Punch-and-Judyish) still delights the unsophisticated with its traditional obscenities. A leading director until lately with the City's Municipal Theatre organization—Tunç Yalman—told me that just as it was the Armenians who were the prime movers in bringing public opera to the City, so with the Western theatre in its turn, the Armenians were the impresarios, and the players too (I speak of theatre, not opera), playing of course in Turkish. At first boys played the female roles, but after a while Ottoman audiences were ready to see women in the roles, provided always that the women were non-Muslims. The public immodesty of Infidel women would not count—my comment, not Tunç Yalman's. So Armenian women were to take the stage. At the turn of the century or thereabouts numbers of young Ottomans of solidly correct background were to become stage-struck. It was happening elsewhere in the civilized world, why not in the City too? Some young Ottomans even became actors themselves. The consequences of this were both odd and significant: the impeccably establishment quality of these young Ottomans' diction at once made the Armenian accent of the ladies playing opposite them so outlandish that the scene would come near to collapsing into farce. It was inevitable that Ottoman public opinion, devoted by now to the Western theatre, and as always to the Turkish language, must in time give in—and we have Muslim girls coming forward as actresses. Today girls from all levels of society become actresses, and I would say that the theatre is the most go-ahead and exciting expression of the City's current artistic life.

The cinema is more prolific than the theatre, and addressed to the country's most prolific element, the Anatolian peasants, who love the rousing wide-screen epics of their past (Seljuk, Ottoman) and the village dramas of their present, in which young girls get terribly threatened with thrashings and worse by middle-aged villains behind huge moustaches. Their saviours, just before the worst befalls, are young men with small moustaches or even none (Plate 26). Pearl White would have understood. Such films make a lot of money, which is not to say that the theatre makes none. On the contrary. Yet the best managements admit little compromise in their choice of play, often enough a foreign import in translation. Managements are rewarded in this policy by full houses for Shaw, Brecht, Ionesco, Beckett, Wesker, Arthur Miller, all the names we know, and of course Shakespeare as well as works by Turkish playwrights, but a six-week run will normally exhaust the City's potential audience for such plays. Standards of acting are extremely high. Yildiz Kenter is an actress we may compare only with the finest we know elsewhere. She is in management with her brother, Müsfik Kenter, himself a fine actor. Another management to look out for is the Dormen. Visitors can safely choose blind—a Kenter, a Dormen, or, say, a

Gülriz Sururi/Engin Çessar production, particularly if any one
of them is doing a modern musical. It will be done on a shoestring
and with tremendous vigour, and the unknown Turkish words
won't matter.

Perhaps it is that the City itself is (and always has been) a
theatre for the performance of history. Yesterday's Ottomans,
with their genius for causing others to work brilliantly in their
name, can be thought of as, at once, impresario and audience,
the players being the slaves they directed so well. By the end of
the seventeenth century, however, the production had gone stale,
the *Enderun*-pages could no longer be depended on to give a good
performance. A thorough-going change of cast was needed, and
the languages of foreign diplomacy were needed too—French,
Italian. An Ottoman would not demean himself by learning infidel
tongues. So the wealthy, well-established Greek community
down in the Phenar quarter on the Golden Horn were brought
in to fill the various new roles, such as Dragoman ('Inter-
preter') of the Sublime Porte, equivalent of Foreign Minister, or
nearly; or Hospodar (viceroy, effectively) of Wallachia and Mol-
davia. The Greek holder of such appointments would often have
completed his studies at an Italian university such as Padua. These
were the 'Phenariots'. Each of them in turn would have had to
buy himself in—the 'donative' again—much as the sultan had to
buy himself into the good graces of his Janissaries on his accession.
And the Phenariot would risk being kicked out again, sometimes
quite soon and for no better reason than that the sultan was short
of gold once more and proposed to put himself in funds by a
change of minister and the new man's entrance fee. This was something everybody from the sultan downwards perfectly understood
and would make provision against; but in fact far fewer of these
Phenariots than has been asserted seem to have made hay im-
moderately while their uncertain sun still shone. In effect they
ruled the Ottoman Empire for generations, loyally and well, till
the Greek War of Independence from the Turks (1822) drew near,
and (their loyalty divided now) they could no longer be relied
upon to dance to the Ottoman tune. The achievement of these
Phenariots in the sultan's service till then had been applauded by
their masters with no hint of envy. It was taken to be Ottoman

achievement, rather as in twentieth-century England the works of a Delius or a T. S. Eliot are taken to be English.

But with the Phenariots gone (to Greece, at long last independent) and the *Enderun* school closed down, who was available both trustworthy and capable of playing the leading roles for the sultan?

Providentially Sultan Mahmut II, himself strong and capable, had set about a programme of 'Westernizing' reforms. For the first time in Ottoman history since the Fall education and opportunities were given to the country's native-born sons; so that Mahmut's successor, Abdul Mecit I, could be guided by Turkey's first real native-born statesman, Mustafa Reshid Pasha, with his *Tanzimat* system of political reforms. And when Abdul Aziz succeeded in 1861 there was another, even greater, trained native-born statesman to guide him—Midhat Pasha, 'Father of the Turkish Constitution'. But Abdul Aziz sank back again into the old familiar patterns of sloth and extravagance, despotism, exiles without trial. The bowstring for sultans was a thing of the past by now, but Midhat Pasha secured instead a *fetva* from the Grand Mufti that deposed the sultan, who in his misery opened a vein in his wrist with a pair of nail-scissors and died. Another *fetva* deposed his successor Murat V three months later, making way for Sultan Abdul Hamid II—'Abdul the Damned'—he too was destined to be deposed, but not before his country had been damned with him. All power flowed back from the Sublime Porte to the palace once again, into the hands of a court favourite, soon to be Grand Vizier. The sultan set aside the Constitution with the comment that the people were unfitted for parliamentary government. Midhat Pasha was exiled; and in due course strangled in his distant lonely prison by orders of the sultan—the last Grand Vizier to meet this fate on his sultan's orders. Under such sultans as these—old men with ideas even older—the country's finances went from bad to worse, till the only way out was the Trusteeship of the Public Debt, 'the Ottoman Debt', which empowered creditor nations to reimburse themselves from the taxes and the customs receipts; all this to the murmuring first of the Young Ottomans, growing nearer with the Young Turks (significantly named), armed risings, a mounting sense of nationhood, of

'Turkishness', Mustafa Kemal, soon to become Atatürk, 'Father of the Turks'. At last the Turks were themselves to play their own leading roles.

As spring advances into summer the City will be busy changing its skin. Many more people than you might think could afford two homes will be moving from one little house in the City to another little house up the Bosphorus or away on one of the Princes' Islands in the Sea of Marmara. The theatres will be closing, all the resources of the Municipal Theatre circuit (eight theatres in all) will be concentrating on Shakespeare season in the open-air theatre of Rumeli Hisar—unless the 1966 new brooms in the organization have completely changed its traditions. The new Istanbul Opera House (nearing £3 million, ten years in the building, a veritable civic centre of all the arts) is confidently promised to the public this year, next year, some time. . . . The public rage, the Opera House stares emptily, glassily back at them on Taksim Square. And meanwhile the City's opera company will be playing a summer season at the open-air theatre near the Hilton Hotel. The Kenters will be off to play summer-stock in distant Anatolian villages, a succession of gruelling one-night stands that for an hour or two will raise the peasants they play to into a world that seems bigger than their own poverty-stricken little village.

Tourists will be arriving.

There are plenty of summer things to do. Most of them scarcely need to be pointed out—sightseeing, trips up the Bosphorus by water-bus, stopping off at some village jetty like a Victorian wooden summerhouse. Waterside restaurants, cafés under plane trees, the Black Sea to bathe in or just to look out over so as to say you've seen it. The organized bathing-beaches (at Ataköy, popular; or Florya, somewhat chic-er) are excellent for people who like everything laid on for them. Others will picnic beside the dams here called 'Bends' up in the Belgrade Forest, or in some water-meadow in a landscape made even more lyrical by great Byzantine or Ottoman aqueducts to span the valleys between the rolling wooded hills. The Muslim cemeteries up above Üsküdar across the water draw many with fat laden baskets of food and fruit. Cemeteries here are not in the least sad places, probably because Muslims do not fear death and so do not have to show him a silent, slightly shamefaced respect; but for those who do fear him and yet want an excuse for walking through the lovely cemeteries there, then let their objective be a mosque near by, the beautiful little Çinili Camii, built for Kössem Valide in 1640. Go in and say a prayer for her soul. Avoid perhaps the Princes' Islands at week-ends when the empty wooded coasts will be stuffed to capacity—like the useful taxi-*dolmuş*.

And now I must announce that nothing of the agreeable sort that I have been proposing is likely to happen soon enough to prevent something very disconcerting from happening first.

The ship was late the first time I came to the City. Darkness had fallen long before it was in sight. We foreigners aboard were grumbling amongst ourselves. Not only had we been deprived of the first breathtaking view from the sea, but there had been a magnificent sunset that ought by rights to have back-lit the City's skyline for us as we sailed into port. It had back-lit the Dardanelles instead, and this was not thought to be at all the same thing. What follows now ought to have opened the book; but the business of writing is unlike the business of travel in that a writer can play tricks with the running order of his experience and a traveller cannot. A writer *must* sometimes cheat, in fairness to his subject as well as to his readers. I have cheated by keeping something back.

Night arrival. All cats are grey at night, all ports identical. All lights on docks are lonely and in customs sheds hostile. Tired, flustered, deprived; strength only to withstand the crowds and watch the customs officer's merciful quick chalk marks. An unfamiliar currency to fumble in for porters' tips. Taxis importune outside, with their black-white, yellow-white chequered bands at window level. The taxi-man has not put down the flag, you are as putty in his hands, he intends to charge ten, fifteen *liras* for a trip it said in 'All you need in Turkey', or wherever it was you read it, should not be more than five. The taxi-man addresses himself to the shortest route.

The shortest route from the docks to a Beyoğlu hotel, the newcomer's obvious destination, is up a precipice. Cobblestones glint

like anthracite, there is an awareness of streets climbing narrow
as ravines to some towering watershed, with sudden blanks—
erosion? Gaps between old people's teeth?—up up up an ancient
airshaft into lodging-house land as grey as the putty-coloured
hands we wring (Plate 22). Here and there a blaze of poisoned
neon, bile green, sick yellow (though don't blame Beyoğlu for
that), and then a two-lane curving boulevard makes promise of
the twentieth century and hastily withdraws it. An impression
of transience, of dark squalor, the traffic silent but for the thump
of wheels on cobbles, traffic like avengers, something terrible
is going to happen. . . .

It has not happened yet but you know it will as you lie in your
hotel bed and listen to the tragic night outside, night filled with
whistlings and the ring-rang of iron-shod staves crying out for
help, threatening each other—how are you to know that you
should love these mournful whistlings, these metallic threats, as
all Turkish children love them? It is the *bekçi-baba*s, night-watch-
men, ring-ranging with their staves, whistling, watching over you
in the dark, communicating with each other in their own sad,
distant way. Péra-Beyoğlu, this first glimpse of it, the sight and
sound of it, I must say it once and for all, it is *awful*! Some visitors
never recover; all have cried it out aloud: '*La Spleen de Péra!*',
Robert Liddell quoting Stephen Spender deliberately out of con-
text (but only just)—'The City builds its horror in my brain . . .' [1]
—lovely phrase, poor Péra.

Madame de Sévigné wrote that the King of France's First
Maître d'Hôtel was reporting on the looks of the Princess of
Bavaria who had just arrived in France to be the Dauphin's bride.
He said: 'Sire, sauvez le premier coup d'œil et vous en serez fort
content.' ('Do not judge at first sight and you will be well pleased
with her.') By now Péra-Beyoğlu is dear to me. And she is *not*
ugly, dirty, squalid, except in so far as all cities are ugly, dirty,
squalid. She is only said to be, just as many of us are said to be
hideous, but the fact is hotly denied by our loved ones. I behold
Péra-Beyoğlu as a beauty now, but this does not, alas, mean that

---

[1] From *Poems*, London, 1933: and Mr Spender tells me that the line can
refer to any big city.

I can shirk my duty to speak out. Beyoğlu is a dear but scruffy and terribly disfigured friend. And while still in this mood of defiant revelation there is something else to add, something in store for the newcomer that is even more disconcerting, because it will strike at the very roots of his self-esteem, and that is where he is most vulnerable.

I was exposed to it for the first time on Istiklal Caddesi, 'Independence Street', 'La Grande Rue de Péra' of the bygone Capitulation Days.

A nineteenth-century canyon, too narrow for the air to get in, too narrow for its function, which is to be all things to all men—shops, theatres, cinemas, *gazinos*, *pavyons* (Fr. *pavillons*), *strip-tiz*, girlie-bars, through one-way traffic conduit and the lure of jaywalkers (Plate 20). The traffic rages one way up the centre and the people are mostly corralled off from the stampede, much as in Pamplona spectators are corralled off when the bulls are let loose on the town. But the jolly fiesta bulls of Pamplona are run but once a year, and on Istiklal Caddesi the stampede is a constant.

All this may be different only in degree from what we suffer in any other helplessly dirty old city that grew up in a horse-drawn, less hysteric age than ours—and there is something even awesome about the horror of its Capitulations architecture, the great rigid ironwork daisies of its *art-nouveau* (Plate 17), the water-lily roots of twisted metal that could squeeze the life out of a man as easily as could an iron boa-constrictor. Immense show-girl caryatids stand at the entrance to arcades, placidly forlorn in their capes of crusted pigeon droppings.

But for any male newcomer (the rules are absolutely different for newcomer girls) no longer insulated from reality by a taxi's body interposed, for anyone on foot, alone, there is a difference in kind as well as in degree, a new and horrifying experience. One's absolute exclusion, rejection. Down the long sad length of this dark tube of a street not a man, woman or child to bear witness to one's presence amongst them, by a look, an inadvertent jostle, even a word in anger at being jostled. One is invisible, non-existent, only 'they' exist. Noted: women safe in head-scarves worn as if they were the discountenanced veils of yesterday; a girl, more than one, with eyes excitingly too pale for the colour of her skin; peasants in other people's breeches; a knee-sized child in a black smock carrying school books and affronting the traffic as Moses did the Red Sea (with equal success, moreover; the traffic curtsies to a shuddering halt, banked solid before the little tot). Noted, then, that the City's traffic is without vice. Noted: every stratum of town and country life is here from the affluent to the heartbreaking poverty of men too proud to beg. Exceptions: the blind and the maimed, to whom begging is permissible. The City's main street looks like other cities' back streets. All this is noted instantly—but oneself remains unnoted, absolutely ex-cluded, though by accident an eye is caught, and instantly averted, like not catching the auctioneer's in sale rooms. Yet every-body is aware of a presence, a foreign presence, by radar, so that 'they' step aside to let the invisible foreigner go by. I would sooner exist to get jostled and to make contact in a succession of apologies.

I spoke of this experience later to various Turks. They were frankly unbelieving; yet it was true—the first few times; and it will be true for every man at first, if he is alone. I stared. I remember thinking: all these people—they don't even look like Turks!

What should Turks look like? I supposed that they would have faces like flat shields. In profile the cheek-bones would lie right up under the eye sockets, from which the flesh would depend in a straight uncurving line to the jawbone—but with a forward tilt so that the nose, neat and fine as paper sculpture, could be set in a true vertical. The eyes would be dark and narrow, heavily lashed, with a hint or more of the Mongolian 'fold' to the eyelid. The skin would be parchment, and if there were any colour in the cheeks it would be russet. Hair? Black bracken. I would also have allowed the admixture of big heavy men with tubular bodies, because I had seen photographs of Turkish wrestlers. And what do I see instead?

I shall be more readily believed if I quote an expert again— Geoffrey Lewis,[1] himself quoting the outcome of an anthropo-morphic investigation carried out in 1937, a sample study, a

[1] London, 1955.

mere 64,000 Turkish souls, but of this sample only 14 per cent of the men (17 per cent of the women) had dark eyes, and blue was not uncommon; only 5 per cent had the Mongolian 'fold' to the eyelid; only 30 per cent had dark hair, medium brown to light brown being commonest. So on this and other evidence the investigators concluded that Turks are 'an Alpine people with a dinaric sprinkling'. For myself, the sample 64,000 souls milling up and down Istiklal Caddesi, men, women, children, were very much like us, but like us presenting our passport-photograph faces, closed minimum faces, set, even uglified deliberately, unshared, designed to give nothing away to anybody—and to conceal, as I now know, inquisitiveness as passionate as my own. But inquisitiveness is vulgar, the Turk is a gentleman, a gentleman does not stare—at least he may not be caught out staring.

The exception to all this is staring at girls, which is permissible. This is no city of wolf whistles that get no one anywhere and are not designed to. Turks staring at girls means what the stare suggests; and where it concerns a foreign girl (all of whom are well known to be no better than prostitutes you need not pay) the prudent girl remembers this, so as to have no disappointments in human nature.

For all that the City's sexuality is carefully concealed from its visitors (not being girls alone), it is there all right. Young men yearn for the girls they can get only in the Hogarthian back-street brothels of a licensed area, such as the one down near the Tower of Galata with a police picket at the baffle-walls of its entrance. Perhaps misguided authority will close this place when the Tower of Galata reopens its doors as a tourist centre with panoramic restaurant and cafeteria and the rest of it, but meanwhile behind the baffle-walls a tremendously brisk turnover is the reward of industry. Quite different are the gipsy girls who tell young men's fortunes on benches, behind bushes, in Taksim Gardens; nor are they really very satisfactory—they just pocket their little fee and return unsmirched to brother or husband or baby waiting on the far side of the bush. What the lonely-heart young man is buying here is five minutes of forgetfulness, five minutes of a warm young woman's attention, addressed exclusively to himself. She is perhaps the only girl he can talk to in the whole long empty

H

day. It is still only at sophisticated levels that there can be an easy amateur relationship between young men and girls. (Plate 24.)

Here in the City there is little contact with visitors who arrive unrecommended, and no casual contact that does not arise naturally from the circumstances, or can be artificially induced from them. Exception: Turkish students/foreign students. But I talk of the rest of us for the rest of our lives. An engaging smile as you approach some respectable stranger with a request for help (the time, the way?) is no part of such inducement. Smiles, unless for reasons already shared, are not the thing at all. A Turkish friend commenting on this said: 'I would wonder what you were laughing at—whether perhaps my flies were undone or something.' So, no ingratiating smiles: they seem as mad here as solitary laughter does to us, and as embarrassing.

How, then, make human contact with the City if you dare not make the first move, and 'they' will not? You *must* make the first move, unsmilingly, and risk that those of the appropriate accosted sex will think you are trying to pick them up in your clumsy way, when all you seek is some assurance that you still exist.

In a down-town *raki*-bar,[1] sawdust, crowded, I stood with an English friend on our silent English island, in our detective-sergeant mackintoshes, suspect, *incomunicado*, and I dropped my glass from nerves. *Flash!* Instantly arms about my shoulders, another glass of *raki* in my hands, words of comfort—I mean words that sounded comforting—and someone with a cucumber begging me to accept it (which could never happen in Greece, and not because the Greeks are a whit less generous). Is this the key, the combination that opens the City's inner doors, is it as simple as this—drop your *raki* glass and let them see how hopelessly lost you are? To shelter the benighted stranger is enjoined upon a Muslim. It is natural for the Turk to be generous when he can see that you are in need. His generosity can even be embarrassing when you can see for your part that he cannot afford it. For he carries over into the city streets the strictly formal rules of hospitality that belong to the mountains and the deserts, the suc-

---

[1] *İçkili* placarded outside a place promises alcoholic drinks inside it: tea- and coffee-shops serve none.

couring of the stranger within his gates. He is by nature open-
handed, warm, friendly, modest, kind and diffident. To break
down the barrier of public social usage here he will need to know
that despite our jaunty gait and air of self-assurance (not to speak
of our outrageous ways), I was—perhaps you will be—we are lost
and bewildered in this City of his, till the *raki* glass gets broken
or we fall and break our legs, or whatever else it is that shatters the
bullet-proofing.

Things are changing in the City, and paradoxically they are
changing even faster in the small Turkish townships and touristic
centres on the west and south coast of Anatolia. Yet it is not a
paradox: the impact of a given weight of tourism is far more
immediate and violent in a small place than it can be in a huge,
amorphous, cosmopolitan city like Istanbul. Tourists coming
back from visits to little places on the west and southern coasts
will be telling me how wrong I am in my conclusions. Perhaps
they will have accepted the formal hospitality of penniless vil-
lagers and mistaken it for friendship won for them by their own
blue eyes. Yet even in the City things are changing fairly rapidly
now. The younger generation mostly do not know that their
grandparents of the Kaiser-war period called the English soldiers
of the 1918 Occupation 'John Kikirik' in derisive onomatopoeic
reference to what was thought of as their giggling ways—but that
does not mean that empty smiles are any the less frowned upon
today. Tourism is going to take its toll: a special category of
Turk will be the outcome, an ingratiatingly smiley Turk, a type
we shall recognize immediately from his counterpart no matter
where. We must try not to deserve him. He will be standing about
near the hotels we stay in, waiting for foreigners. He will be
dressed more chic-ly than his fellow citizens, in a client's cast-
offs perhaps. The City is still in the pre-Marks & Spencers, pre-
Bloomingdales era, pre-Rag Trade. Cheap clothes look cheap and
are badly made, as in pre-war London. This too is slowly changing
here, with a start in excellent low-priced woollen knitted goods,
and the men are better turned out than the girls. But this young
man, lolling against the railings, waiting, is neat as a pin, and his
eyes are like pins, and he has learnt 'Hullo-Joe' English. And
those who are naturals for the Hullo-Joes—which means the

nicest of us, the kindest-hearted, the least suspicious—will be leaving the City, as they left London, Paris or New York or wherever wasn't theirs, saying to the nastiest amongst us, the most wary and doubting, me, I suppose: 'Well, I was lucky, you see—you know, running into that Turkish friend I was telling you about, the very first morning, imagine! You know—to have had someone who could show me the *real* city.'

Chapter 11

Tomorrow

SOMETHING has been happening in recent years that is well on the way to changing the City's entire metabolism—an invasion of peasants from the villages of Anatolia, lured to the city whose 'streets are paved with gold' as their counterparts were lured to Dickens's London. Istanbul is going through its Light Industrial Revolution. This explains why the poverty and underemployment most cities have by now contrived to master, or else to sweep delicately under carpets, is here for all to see, on Istiklal Caddesi as in the back streets. Factories have sprung up all over the hinterland, shanty after shanty springs up in the night, following the lead of tens of thousands that already form the shanty towns they here call *gecekondu*s. Mushrooming and proliferating, they suffix each other, agglutinate like the language, huddle for warmth and human contact. Sun up, the roof is on! The squatter family just arrived is now safe under it—safe, because the authorities are powerless to evict or enforce demolition once the roof is on, unless alternative accommodation can be found, and of course it cannot be. According to a government publication of June 1963 outlining the First Five-Year Development Plan's scope and intentions for 1963–7, 21 per cent of the City's population was even then living in *gecekondu*s. New arrivals from Anatolia at present are averaging some 80,000 annually, Anatolian fertility is startling, almost indecent, in a good year 30 per 1,000 increase. By 1964

40 per cent of the City's population was the unproductive 'under-fifteens' group. The State Planning organization urges the State to authorize at last the use of contraceptives, at present illegal, and to set afoot the necessary Citizens' Advice Bureaux that could indoctrinate citizens in a field that will seem to them as curious as electronics, before the situation gets completely out of hand. Meanwhile the planners have a blueprint for channelling all new industry to the Izmit area, sixty miles distant across the Sea of Marmara, in Asia. Before ever the migrating peasants reach the City they are to be caught and screened off where space exists for them and where there will be work for them as well. But blueprints take time to become realities, and this one perhaps takes too little into account the invading procession-beetles' own ideas. The invaders are making for the City itself, and for nowhere else. They know because they *know* that it is paved with gold, and once they have breathed its laden air, looked out on the city view of life from the doorway of a leaky cardboard shack (but safe—ah! blessed relief!—under their own roof since dawn that day), they can never go home to the village paved with mud, nor to the back-breaking toil, no water in summer, no heat in winter, no light, perhaps no school. And their old folk will be following them soon, because where else can old people die but with their loved ones? It is touching and pitiful. Those who want to know what sort of lives these peasants, even today, are leaving behind them may read *A Village in Anatolia* (*Bizim Köy*) by a Turkish peasant, Mahmut Makal,[1] product of a remarkable experiment in rural education. I can speak of it only from hearsay. It was designed to give village boys and girls a grounding in reading, writing and the absolutely basic technical skills that their future lives as peasants working the land required. These young trainees were then returned to their villages to set up little Village Institutes of their own, and to spread their newly gained knowledge. Inevitably these young people came up against the old traditional leaders of village life, the *Imam*, nearest equivalent in Islam of the priesthood, and the *Hoca*, the religious teacher; and with the fall of the Inönü government, the incoming government preferred to support the old-time village régime rather than the new young.

[1] London, 1954.

The Village Institute scheme that might with luck have succeeded
brilliantly was virtually abandoned.

The peasants see no future for themselves in the village, but
here in the City there will at least be a future for their children—
that is what they say. Too often illiterate themselves, they confidently plan that their children shall go to the *Université*. They
know the word all right. They are good citizens, as good as the
very poor can ever be from the point of view of authority: they
are responsive to discipline, they are decent, clean—the public
*hamam*s are full of them, this is their luxury, the wonderful extravagance of a body steaming clean, even if it has to be put straight
back into the same old shirt and breeches and coat.

Professor Hart, a one-man, one-room experimental Department
of Social Anthropology in the University of Istanbul, has been
conducting a systematic inquiry into the life of one of the older
*gecekondu*s. He is of course prejudiced (who isn't, where the City
is concerned?) and he says that these Anatolian immigrants are
not only to become, as all can see, the City's largest single element,
but are also potentially the City's most valuable citizens, an idea
that must cause old-time citizens to gasp in horror. I have been in
some of their home-made homes. The village mother squats at ease
on the carpet, the City son lounges on a seat, at ease, the young
wife serves minute cups of tea with the urbanity of a real hostess.

Necdet Bey—Bay Necdet Uğur, to give him his post-independ-
ence honorific 'Mister' and surname that no one uses at all—
Necdet Bey, then, one-time Chief of Police, one-time Mayor of
Istanbul, knows all about it. It was he who had the vision to
sponsor the *Çocuk Bürosu* ('children's bureau') so as to catch the
children of 'bad homes'—or simply the children left to their own
devices by *gecekondu* parents who both must go out to work each
day—while still in the pre-delinquent stage. There may be little
or no organized crime in the City, and no juvenile delinquency
to speak of (yet), but perfect breeding grounds for these things
exist among the newcomer Anatolians. Necdet Bey chose an
excellent woman to run his Children's Bureau—the pilot for a
network of such bureaux. She is Nuran Sayın. She gave up a
career as a lawyer to do this for him, and went to the Metropolitan
Police in London for training. Certain of the City's police officers

who then laughed discreetly ('Is it time to feed those children their breakfast, Nuran Sayin?') laugh less perhaps today, because these small beginnings are already bearing fruit. I have seen children come to Police Headquarters of their own accord, children you might expect would fear the very word *Polis*; sometimes it is just a social visit, to sit with one of Nuran Sayin's hand-picked team of workers, who are girls very often, or perhaps to do some scribbling with chalks, or it could be to complain angrily of a drunken father and 'can something be done about it, please, *at once*!' A big stone sitting on Nuran Sayin's desk was found in a little girl's pocket—to hurl, if she could, if any of her father's drunken layabout friends who came to spend the night in their one small room should awake and try something. But they were mostly too drunk, I dare say. Anyway she has no longer any need of her stone, this 'little old woman of nine', and Nuran Sayin can use it for a paper-weight.

Though the suggestion that God could possibly have had need of rest from his labours on the Seventh Day is most offensive to Muslims, Atatürk brought the Turkish week into line with international practice by making the Turkish *Pazar* (our Sunday) the day of rest for Man. Friday was to remain, as always in Islam, the day the Faithful would meet together for the communal prayers. Both the word for Friday (*Cuma*) and the word for the mosque they would meet in (*Cami*) derive from the Arabic root meaning 'congregate'. In the years that followed upon independence, congregations at the City's Friday-mosques were to drop off sharply under the frowns of Atatürk and the secularists. In the villages, as might be expected, Islam proved less easily assailable and has continued to impose its beloved ritual on the peasants' lives. Now that the City itself is being overrun by peasants, both the Friday-mosques and the lesser mosques draw much bigger numbers once again. Some have called the refilling of the mosques 'The Black Reaction'. Others, with little shops and customers whose needs must be considered, have begun closing them quietly on Fridays and opening in secret on Sundays, if they can get away with it.

The citizens snatch at their day of rest, and of a summer Sunday the boats that go battling against the currents of the Bosphorus or fleeing before them are stuffed with pleasure-seekers. Anatolian peasants, now citizens—those 'in work' at least—will be aboard in force. Those not 'in work' will perhaps be visiting a favourite lunatic asylum and talking to the inmates, sharing cigarettes with them, perhaps, all in an enclosure that also contains peacocks and deer and trees. No entrance fee. The Gul Hane zoo under Topkapi Saray charges for entry, naturally enough.

For those 'in work' the Sunday suit, the shoeshine and the shave—in that order of priority. The family is laden. The mother will be carrying a water-flask and the food in its clattering tin containers (often plastic now); also the carpet and a hard bright flowery pillow. Each child will carry something suited to its size, in its mouth the Sunday lollipop. Father carries his chaplet, probably a small affair of eleven up-to-date plastic (or even reconstituted amber) beads, instead of the thirty-three or the sixty-six or the full-scale one hundred and one to name the hundred attributes of Allah and to number the one that is unknowable. He will have passed this little eleven-beaded loop over his middle finger, so that with a quick flick of the wrist he can send it flicking across the back of his hand from under the thumb to behind the little finger. And back again. An agreeable pursuit. With his free hand he may perhaps carry the kettle, should no child of his yet be tall enough to lift it clear of the ground. On the water-bus the mother will watch over the children like a hen, the father will sit placidly immobilized in sleep or something like it. When he rests himself he seems to die, without ever stiffening into death. His body flows like some viscous fluid over whatever is handy or comfortable, a seat back, someone's shoulder (Plate 3). Who else (except the Negro, whom the Turk in no other way resembles) can achieve this wonderful repose?

Beykoz up the Bosphorus might be the destination. Or else some village south down the Asian coast, or perhaps near Sariyer in Europe, or wherever it was the notices tacked to trees in the old city's gathering-places said the Grand Wrestling Tourney was to be held this summer Sunday, 1 p.m. A sort of travelling fair will have set up its canvas screens round some grassy plot, under trees, water handy. Picnickers will be demanding water for the replenishing of their flasks. Streams and springs will supply it;

or one of the lovely fountains they call *çeşme* (built as an act of charity by some rich man of the past). The Turkish forms of wrestling—*güreş*—is still the great national sport, though it is slowly giving in to *futbol*. Today it will be largely amateur contenders.

Mother prepares the picnic, the kids play. Father will be queue-ing up for the wrestling. People who lack the entrance fee may look around for a handy tree near by to climb and watch from. Inside it is a predominantly male audience. There will be a band at the entrance or just outside, a shrill reed instrument, perhaps two, and a thumping big drum the drummer may have a mind to dance with from time to time. Together they will dispense the Turkish folk music that was held by Bela Bartok, who came to study it, to be the richest in his experience, both melodically and rhythmically.

The wrestlers are naked but for black leather breeches, cut as low as bikinis round the groin, and fitting as tightly as a cutter's art can manage. They finish off below the knee with a bandage and a frill of leather. Geometric patterns decorate these breeches in bold overstitching, for beauty. The wrestlers oil themselves plentifully—also each others' backs. Their bodies are hard and taut and tubular (as I had foreseen) and not in the least like the postur-ing, pot-bound, hothouse flowers of Muscle Beach and the physique magazines. They are presented to the audience by an impresario, their right arms raised, their faces set like those of sultans ignoring ambassadors. They will have been paired off, the fights will be simultaneous, all over the arena, perhaps a dozen pairs. But first a solemn Dance of Challenge. They plunge and they thump across the grass in slow motion. Elephantine. Their gestures are deliberately ponderous and rounded (Ottoman, perhaps?), they bend the knee like courtiers, but not to us, they bow the head to Mother Earth, touching her, silently seeking her support in the battle that is com-ing now, they pluck a blade of grass and munch it ritually. As they pass each other they may mime a 'hold', they will clinch sometimes, one man's arms around another's waist, working them up and down the oily cylinder of the torso like piston-rings. Then it begins. It will finish only when in due course one of each pair has been floored, whereupon a second wave of wrestlers will take the place of the first, and perhaps a third the place of the second. It all takes a very, very long time. Father will be hungry for his food when it is over at last.

In English village cricket players borrow cricket bats and pads if they haven't got their own. In Turkish village-*güreş* many amateur wrestlers have to borrow breeches for the same reason. Since there are no dressing-rooms and the breeches are the only garment worn, and since no second-wave borrower can get into them (or the occupier out of them) without for that moment offending against the Koran's puritanically strict nakedness taboos, for this once stark public nakedness is permissible, but it must be brief. In the segregation of the Turkish public *hamam*s (bathhouses), whereas women are not required to cover up at all (or so women have assured me), men must always be 'careful not to show any immodest parts'—as the *Enderun*-page Bassano warned us centuries ago: 'For shameless ones are beaten and thrown out.' Here on the village grass what ought not to happen, does happen, yet has *not* happened. The inevitable offence is calmly ignored. Inevitable, also, that the borrowed breeches will not really fit. They are mostly far too large—for who could even get into breeches far too small? Over-large breeches put the wearer to a hideous disadvantage. Apart from the arm locks that can keep two heaving, well-oiled men solidly on their four feet, there seem to be no holds more solid than those on an opponent's waist-band. But what if the waist-band is too loose? In village-*güreş* the extraordinary consequence is that a wrestler will make a dive for his opponent's crutch, back or front, as available, plunging the arm deep inside the waist-band, whereupon (if he can get it right) he has his enemy immobilized. We now see why they were all so busy oiling inside their breeches as well as out. This does not, however, answer our alarmed unspoken questions. I have been forced to ask Turkish friends to explain. They were surprised, and a little worried; they said they had never seen or heard of such a thing and that I must be gravely mistaken. Perhaps they had watched only professional *güreş* (which for some reason I have never seen). There, no doubt, everyone's leather breeches would have been made to measure and would fit far too tightly for the village crutch-hold that so startles the innocent foreigner. I took an Englishwoman with me one Sunday. She sat silent and astonished and in the end quite lost her head and cried out loud: 'But what are they *doing* to each other?' What indeed? It is exactly what I had begged my Turkish friends

to tell me. I have had to fall back on deductions. Here is my
explanation. No other would last ten seconds in the arena or in
terms of good sense. *This* is what you have to do. Plunge the arm
in, hook the hand or wrist round the enemy crutch. Your fore-
arm has now become lever to the fulcrum of the waist-band that
it stretches tight. Now—if you can only get it right—your oily
enemy may heave and thump like a sea-lion but you have him in
an almost unbreakable hold and he must stay long minutes ignominiously up-ended, if you so choose (Plate 25), till rage or dis-
honour or a moment of boredom or inattention on your part
lends him the skill to extricate himself. Better sit down now quickly
in the grass in the honey-pot position before he upends you in
revenge.

The happy hours pass, the audience lolls and squats, spreads
itself, watching, not watching, munching grass, drinking *Kola-
Koka* (*sic*), amalgamated into one great entity in which we foreigners (if only few in number) become fused, a wordless part
of what is going on, part of the slow warm companionship that
seems to come naturally to Turks among themselves. Smiles—
of companionship and something shared—are now allowed. The
closed excluding faces of Istiklal Caddesi have somehow opened
up like flowers. Can they really be the same people who denied
our very existence? But we are part of it now; and later, rather
tired, and stiff with the unaccustomed squatting, dusty too, we
shall be leaving with pats and handshakes, in our ears the strange
soft words of farewell that here speed the parting friend—*güle
güle!* The water-bus again, hooting; deep water racing past the
summer villages and the old decrepit lovely wooden summer
houses that the Ottoman rich of another day called their *yalis*.

The little journey is rolling itself up again, the Marmara
will be showing on the left beyond Üsküdar, convex, a huge
upturned platter covered with ships sailing home to the City.
To the right, the heights of Beyoğlu dominated by the Tower
of Galata—who dares to call her ugly now? Then the Golden
Horn reveals itself, red-gold under the sun that is setting where
all along we knew it should—behind old Stamboul; and the skyline, back-lit, marches against the curve of our changing course in a
triumphant procession of domes and minarets. This is it. The City.

Index